"Written with rigour, creativity, and the day-to-day insight of a true scientist. [*God in the Lab*] has widened the horizons of the science and faith debate by bringing new and needed perspectives. I heartily recommend it."

Dr Sharon Dirckx, Tutor at the Oxford Centre for Christian Apologetics, author and former brain imaging scientist

"[*God in the Lab*] is both well researched and contains a fresh and inspiring personal narrative. It should reignite in others a passion for the friendship between science and religious belief."

Revd David B. Rowe, Warden of the Lee Abbey Community

"Ruth Bancewicz's beautifully-written book demonstrates how science enhances faith, with many examples from real scientists who are Christians, and many memorable quotations. This is a great book to give to those who believe there is a conflict between science and faith."

Professor Sir Colin Humphreys, Director of Research at Cambridge University and President of Christians in Science

"On a topic so often dominated by the culture wars, Dr Bancewicz brings a fresh and much-needed emphasis on wonder to conversations about science and Christian faith. She reminds us that the beauty, awe, and creativity of the natural world points to its Creator. This readable book would m̲_____student."

I̲ _____ **er and President of BioLogos**

Dr Ruth Bancewicz studied genetics at the Universities of Aberdeen and Edinburgh before working as the Development Officer for Christians in Science, a post she held for three years. She is now a Senior Research Associate at The Faraday Institute for Science and Religion, Cambridge (UK), where she works on positive expressions of the science–faith dialogue and has developed the Test of FAITH resources.

For more articles, videos, and podcasts visit www.godinthelab.org

God in the Lab

How Science Enhances Faith

Ruth M. Bancewicz

MONARCH
BOOKS
Oxford, UK, and Grand Rapids, Michigan, USA

Published by Monarch Books
an imprint of
Lion Hudson plc
Wilkinson House, Jordan Hill Road, Oxford OX2 8DR, England
Email: monarch@lionhudson.com
www.lionhudson.com/monarch

ISBN 978 0 85721 568 0
e-ISBN 978 0 85721 569 7

First edition 2015

Acknowledgments

Scripture quotations taken from the Holy Bible, New International Version, copyright © 1973, 1978, 1984, 2011 International Bible Society. Used by permission of Hodder & Stoughton, a member of the Hodder Headline Group. All rights reserved. 'NIV' is a trademark of International Bible Society. UK trademark number 1448790.
pp. 110–11, 112: Extract from *Living Form of the Imagination* by Douglas Hedley copright © Douglas Hedley, 2008. T&T Clark, by permission of Bloomsbury Publishing Plc.

pp. 131–32: Extract from article "Walking the Walk: Thoreau and the art of seeing nature" by Jeff Hardin in *Books and Culture* copyright © Jeff Hardin, 2013. Reprinted by permission of *Books and Culture*.
pp. 154–55: Extract from *The Weight of Glory* by C.S. Lewis copyright © C.S. Lewis Pte. Ltd. 1949. Reprinted by permission.
pp. 165–66, 177: Extract from *Unweaving the Rainbow* by Richard Dawkins copyright © Richard Dawkins, 1998. Reprinted by permission of Houghton Mifflin Harcourt Publishing Company and Penguin Books. All rights reserved.
p. 174: Extract from *The Sense of Wonder* by Rachel Carson copyright © Rachel L. Carson. Reprinted by permission of Frances Collin, Trustee.
p. 208: Extract from *The God Delusion* by Richard Dawkins copyright © Richard Dawkins, 2007. Reprinted by permission of Houghton Mifflin Harcourt Publishing Company and Random House.
pp. 221, 225: Extract from *From Galileo to Gell-Mann: The Wonder that Inspired the Greatest Scientists of All Time: In Their Own Words* by Marco Bersanelli and Marco Gargantini, originally published in Italy as *Solo Lo Stupore Conosce*, copyright © Marco Bersanelli and Marco Gargantini, 2003. Reprinted by permission of RCS Libri S.p.A., Milan and Templeton Press, Pennsylvania.

A catalogue record for this book is available from the British Library

Printed and bound in the UK, December 2014, LH26

Contents

Foreword

Many books have been written from a faith-friendly perspective, showing how the Christian faith creates intellectual space for the natural sciences. Dr Ruth Bancewicz, a former research biologist, has given us a work that moves this discussion up to a higher level. Her concern is not merely to show that science is consistent with faith, but that science *enhances* faith. This richly documented book weaves together Dr Bancewicz's own experience as a scientist with the stories of other scientists, who have found that their faith was deepened by their research and reflections. These personal narratives convey the rich potential for dialogue and interaction between science and faith far more effectively than reams of reasoned argument.

Readers will find much within these pages that is helpful, stimulating, and challenging. Perhaps the most original and important sections of the work deal with the importance of beauty and the human imagination in both science and the Christian faith. Dr Bancewicz's exploration of these themes opens up lines of thought that will be new to many readers, and has the potential to bring a deepened appreciation of the world which science investigates. It will be warmly welcomed by all those thinking about the relation of science and faith.

Alister McGrath
Andreas Idreos Professor of Science and Religion
University of Oxford

Chapter 1

The Theologian and the Telescope

Science is not threatened by God; it is enhanced.
Francis Collins, former director of the Human Genome Project[1]

*the historical titans of the scientific revolution –
Galileo, Kepler, Bacon, Pascal, and Newton – all
devout believers to a man – could interrelate their
Christian faith and their scientific discoveries.*
Nancy Frankenberry, philosopher of religion[2]

I have always enjoyed science, particularly when it involves studying living things. I have happy memories of wading around rivers and rock pools on high school field trips, encountering microscopic organisms in university lab classes, and examining cells and tissues as a research student. Doing science brings the joy of exploration and the freedom to ask questions. There is a feeling of wonder and awe at what is found and an enjoyment of its beauty. Those moments of discovery raise deeper questions about the universe and our experience of it.

Now that I am working in science and religion for a

living, I have learned that it's important to keep reminding myself about the reality of life in the lab. During any intense discussion about an issue or seeming point of conflict between science and faith, we need to remember what life is like for those who actually do research every day. So I have developed a passion for helping people to enjoy the wonder of the natural world, and see beyond the debates to the more personal or spiritual side of science.

What I hope to achieve in these pages is best illustrated by a story about a theologian and a telescope. The theologian was a colleague from another department in Cambridge, and the telescope belonged to some friends of his. As we sat down to lunch one day, my colleague mentioned that he had visited these friends the night before. It was a clear night, so they had spent some time looking at the stars.

My colleague was a keen amateur astronomer as a teenager, but he had become involved in so many academic debates about science and religion that he eventually lost interest in science. That evening, he was reminded how beautiful and fascinating the universe can be. He realized that the experience of scientific exploration itself can foster awe, wonder, and – for people of faith – worship. As the theologian and former biophysicist Alister McGrath has often said, science points to questions that are too deep and too complex to be answered by science itself.[3]

These experiences of science enhancing faith are not unique. Science has a long tradition of being complementary to Christianity, although that is not always recognized now. The universities in medieval Europe taught both science and theology, and at the time they weren't even necessarily seen as separate subjects. Experiments and field studies were largely carried out by the clergy, and it was only in the nineteenth century that science was established as a separate profession. The occasional points of conflict between science and faith have been well publicized by those who wish to drive a wedge between science and faith. In reality, these debates were not "scientists versus the Church", because science has always been supported from the inside by Christians who are passionate about exploring the universe that God has made.[4]

A recent survey by the American sociologist Elaine Howard Ecklund showed that both faith and spirituality are still thriving in the scientific world. Between 2005 and 2007, Ecklund and her team carried out nearly 1,700 surveys and 275 in-depth interviews with senior scientists in twenty-one elite US universities. Their goal was to paint a more accurate and up-to-date picture of how scientists approach religion, and the results make interesting reading. About 50 per cent of all the people interviewed were members of a specific religious group, and 30 per cent were atheists.[5] The remaining 20 per cent did not believe in God, but valued something beyond science that they chose to call spiritual.[6]

Some of these "spiritual but not religious" scientists had a strong sense of awe and wonder at the natural world. There was a sense of mystery too – a belief that there is something beyond the material. These people found that their spiritual values motivated them to do things differently: to spend more time teaching so that others could share the same experience, to choose what they saw to be more worthwhile fields of research, or to change their behaviour outside of the laboratory. So while there may be some individuals who reject discussions about science and faith, there are plenty of others who are interested in a more thoughtful dialogue.

My own experience of science followed the usual pattern: an early interest that was encouraged by the adults around me, including my Christian parents, followed by years of study and a long apprenticeship in the techniques of laboratory research. There are always a few early-career scientists who decide to leave the lab and follow other science-related vocations, and I realized I was one of these people when I felt myself gravitating towards my desk. I enjoyed reading, writing, and giving presentations, and found that experiments interrupted the flow of my work! It was time for me to leave the lab, but not without some regret at no longer being able to see beautiful things under the microscope.

The unexpected part of my route out of the lab was that it led into science and religion. I was a Christian by the time I arrived at university, so I had joined Christians in Science (CiS): an international organization for those interested in the dialogue between science and faith. My decision to leave science coincided with an advertisement for a CiS staff position, so I instantly applied. A few months later I began to work with science students, lab researchers, and many others, helping to supply them with resources and organize events where various faith-based issues could be discussed.

After several years travelling the length and breadth of the UK with CiS, I moved to The Faraday Institute for Science and Religion in Cambridge, where I now work on the relationship between science and Christianity. I am more than content with my new career outside the lab, but I remain fascinated by science.

My first few years in Cambridge were spent developing *Test of FAITH*, a series of resources to help churches and other groups tackle questions about science and Christianity. During this time I was challenged to recognize that while debates and discussions are important, they're not the whole story. In a video interview, Alister McGrath said that it is also important to start new conversations about how science enhances faith, rather than always responding to issues.[7] So I followed up this idea, was given some generous funding from the Templeton World Charity Foundation to communicate some of these more positive stories, and my blog scienceandbelief.org is part of that work.

This book is the final output of that project, and is an exploration of the experiences in science that can enhance faith. It's also about the human side of science: what drives and motivates us, and what we enjoy. For those scientists who are Christians, their research is simply one expression of a faith that covers every aspect of their life. For many others, science and religion will seem like two separate worlds, and the topics addressed in this book will act as a bridge between the two.

The journey described here is a personal one. Imagination, creativity, beauty, wonder, and awe are all subjects that are close to my heart, and I have thoroughly enjoyed exploring them. I'm not one for travelling alone, so during my writing I have spoken with a number of working scientists who are also Christians. Their stories are included in these pages, reflecting their own unique perspectives on science and faith.

I'll begin by explaining how science works, including the people and their quirks as well as the day-to-day business of research. Practising scientists may wish to skip this chapter, but others will hopefully appreciate a fly-on-the-wall view of life in the laboratory. Next I will explain why I am a Christian, and how I see science and faith fitting together. The trajectory of the rest of the book is through creativity and imagination, which are vital to the practice of both science and Christianity, to the beauty, wonder, and awe that scientists experience in their work, and that (for some) lead beyond science to God.

These pages will contain no arguments for God as such, but are more of a thought experiment, particularly when it comes to beauty, wonder, and awe. If the God of the Bible existed, what would you expect to see in the world? Does viewing the universe through the lens of faith make it look more coherent? I find that what I see in science helps my faith to grow, and enlarges my view of God.

With apologies to social scientists, when I write about "science" here, I mean natural science (e.g. biology, physics, and chemistry). I should also add that this is not intended to be an academic book, although I have referenced plenty of more scholarly works for those who want to follow up particular points. I have touched on some complex issues, and my aim has simply been to share some of what I feel is interesting and valuable, drawing on enough of the thinking of others to start an interesting conversation.

I have noticed that when I throw a topic like beauty or awe into a debate, people start to tell stories and listen to each other. We sometimes concentrate so hard on getting our point across that it's difficult to engage with others, so we need to find some ways to begin again. Like my friend the theologian, it's easy to get lost in abstractions. I hope that these insights gleaned from the laboratory and the library will help to start some dialogues where it's possible to learn from each other and appreciate both the fascination of science and the deeper questions that it raises.

Chapter 2

Life in the Lab

If you want to know how scientists proceed,
do not listen to what they say but watch what they do.
Albert Einstein, theoretical physicist[8]

If we assume we've arrived, we stop searching.
Jocelyn Bell Burnell, astronomer[9]

I like finding out how things work. When I was small I did what all children do, asking "Why?" and "What's that?" all the time, and I never lost the habit. I also enjoy being outdoors. My walks tend to take a long time because I want to stop and look at all the plants and animals I come across. If I have to be inside I tend to bring the outdoors with me, so my home is full of plants, flowers from the garden, and objects I've found on walks and brought back in my pockets. This combination of curiosity and an interest in living things meant that I was drawn to biology.

My sixth form[10] biology teachers had specialized in plant science and genetics, so I went to university with plant genetics in mind. I felt immensely privileged to be spending my days in the library and lecture halls at Aberdeen University, asking "Why?" and "What's that?" to my heart's content. I eventually realized that I preferred studying organisms that move, so I switched to biomedical science, and spent my last few years at university focusing on human genetics and molecular biology.

The human body is a phenomenal self-building, self-healing structure. Its processes are so complex that I half-expected most of them to be beyond understanding, but thankfully I was wrong. In one class we learned about the ear, where sound waves are converted to brain waves through an ingenious system of tiny hairs and vibrating membranes. Muscles had me fascinated too. Each one is a bundle of thousands of interlocking filaments that can move along each other, causing the entire tissue to contract.

The poet W. B. Yeats said that "education is not the filling of a pail, but the lighting of a fire".[11] I think a fair bit of pail-filling is necessary in scientific education, and I enjoyed it immensely (I only recently threw out my first university textbook), but my lecturers managed to light a fire at the same time. They admitted when they weren't sure how something worked, explained the alternative theories, and pointed out gaping holes in current scientific understanding – perhaps these were problems we could work on in the future.

Our practical classes were a bit more pedestrian. We worked through tried and tested protocols, hoping to see what we were told we should see. Looking for the right answers is one way to learn the craft of laboratory work, but it's not always very motivating. We were all too eager to dump everything down the sink or in the bin at the end of the day and dash off to dinner. I'm sure our lecturers tried hard to provide interesting problems for us to tackle, but short of putting us in working research laboratories right from the start (now there's an idea!), it must be nigh on impossible to design interesting experiments for a large and diverse class on a limited budget.

Some of our lab sessions were more interesting. There was the time we watched yeast grow – which probably sounds a bit like watching paint dry, but was an exciting moment for me. Until that point, growth had been something that happened when you weren't looking: a mysterious process too slow to watch. We had learned some of the biochemical processes involved in laying down new cell wall material and expanding the cell's contents, but it was one-dimensional knowledge.

The experiment that helped me to see growth in real-time involved putting some filamentous (thread-like) yeast on a microscope slide and using a microscopic measuring scale to follow the progress of a single filament as it grew. I remember calling my lab partner, Duncan, over: "Look, you can actually see it growing!" He was excited too. Only a biology geek could think a few millimetres of movement is exciting, but that's the whole point of the story. One of the messages I hope to get across in this chapter is what makes a scientist tick.

In our final year we were each given a placement in one of the university research labs where we could work on a project of our choice. I picked cancer research, and spent several weeks scraping cells off microscope slides and analyzing their DNA. I was terrified of collecting the wrong cells or muddling the samples up, but it was exciting to be finally planning my own experiments and looking for answers to new questions.

The purpose of this chapter is not just to share my own

experience, but to give a series of snapshots that demonstrate what really happens in science: the fun parts, the challenges, and the mundane – in other words, the human side of science, and particularly biology because that is what I know best. The first half is about the nuts and bolts of how things work in the lab, and the rest is more philosophical. As I'm no longer based in a lab I'll share my own thoughts alongside those of a working scientist, and I'll do the same for each of the other main chapters.

If you have not been in a lab since school, then this chapter is primarily for you. We hear about scientific discoveries in the news, but we don't often get to find out how those discoveries are actually made. Like most careers, a job in science is very unglamorous but it has its rewards. There is enough interest and excitement to keep researchers coming back to work day after day, putting in the extra hours at evenings and weekends. Hopefully I can help you to appreciate their enthusiasm.

Surprised by science

I wanted the perspective of a more seasoned scientist for this chapter, so I visited Dr Harvey McMahon at the Laboratory of Molecular Biology (LMB) in Cambridge. As I write, the LMB alumnus Michael Levitt has just won a Nobel Prize (the fourteenth LMB member to do so), and no doubt others will follow suit. This is a highly competitive environment, inhabited by some very talented researchers.

Harvey McMahon is interested in the communication between nerve cells in the brain, and how this process can happen so incredibly fast. His work is important for understanding how we think, and neurodegenerative conditions such as Parkinson's disease. Harvey is also a Christian, and I will include that side of his story towards the end of the chapter. I was interested to hear his views on science: what makes good research, what makes a good lab tick, and how it's possible to learn anything new in biology.

My arrival at Harvey's lab coincided with their weekly meeting: a ritual of tea, cake, and research presentations. This week's speaker was an unusual member of the group: a qualified medical doctor and neurologist who had decided to branch into lab-based research. He boldly presented his latest progress, and then his co-workers quizzed him, deconstructing his data piece by piece. He did well, defending his hypothesis and taking every piece of critique on the chin. Some suggested ideas for new experiments, and others questioned his practical techniques and offered advice to help him. The atmosphere was competitive, but the work of the lab was clearly a team effort.

This intimate gathering of colleagues is the first and possibly the most important testing ground for new ideas in science. Every lab I have been to has similar meetings, and the critique they provide is essential. These are the people who know your work inside out, and if you can convince them you have shown something new, then you are most probably on to a good thing. The ambitious young researchers at the LMB would have welcomed evidence disproving the latest theories, especially if it secured their place at a future Nobel banquet.

After the meeting, Harvey gave me a tour of the institute's brand new state-of-the-art building, full of light and space. The lab itself is crowded, but everyone has a place at the bench and a niche in the office. He introduced me to the members of his research group like a proud father, encouraging them to show me their latest data. One person showed me bright photographs of strange cell structures that could have been pieces of art. Others were distracted by experiments – hovering as we talked – ready to complete the next step of the protocol.

What struck me most when I spoke to Harvey is that he seems surprised to find himself being a lab head in a famous research institute. He was the first in his family to go to university, and only then because a "kind old lady" (his words) persuaded his father that he needed to study, and offered to pay for his education. The brain seemed to be something people didn't know very much about, so Harvey decided to study neuroscience.

The other remarkable thing about Harvey is how much he enjoys doing experiments. As the head of a research group it would be normal practice for him to spend most of his time in the office or travelling to conferences, leaving the manual labour to others, but he is much happier at the bench. Seeing him there reminded me of Marie Curie's statement about "that atmosphere of peace and meditation which is the true atmosphere of a laboratory".[12] Harvey said a molecular biology lab is "not peaceful, but I can think. I can't plan an experiment sitting at a desk, but I can if I've got a pipette in my hand."

Meeting Harvey also reminded me about the importance of gratitude. In his book *Culture Making,* the writer and musician Andy Crouch writes about the students he met when he was a campus minister at Harvard University, most of whom fell into one of three groups.[13] The first he called the "strivers". These hard-working people had spent most of their lives preparing for university, and now they were there they scurried around from morning till night with bulging bags on their backs. They had no time for anything but study, and struggled with anxiety.

The second group Crouch observed were the "legacies". These students were supremely confident, feeling entitled through family connections, fortune or fame, to stroll down the halls of Harvard, at home and at ease. Finally comes the smallest group but the most fun to be around: the "children of grace". They hadn't thought they stood a chance of getting into a place like Harvard, but they were delighted to be there. They loved their studies, and continued to be surprised and delighted as they progressed through university, finding time to grow personally as well as learn. They may have been blessed by academic brilliance or easy-going personalities, but these contented students were also very grateful to be at Harvard and were going to make the most of every opportunity.

The people who tend to stick with science as a career and do well are often the ones who can't believe anyone would pay them to do something as fun as play around in a lab. There might be dry periods or the stress of bidding for funding, but in between are days of exploring the subject they know best. They're surprised to have made it so far, and plan to keep going as long as they can.

Life in the lab

The word "laboratory" can mean two things. A lab is a place: a building, a room or a series of rooms where people do experiments. A lab is also a group of people, because science is almost always a communal activity. More often than not, both meanings of the word apply.

Each lab has its own distinctive atmosphere, but there are some ways of doing things that must be almost universal to science. In many ways, being a research scientist is similar to any other job. You go to work in the morning, and stay as long as you need to. Some aspects of the role are highly enjoyable and some are mundane. In any lab you will encounter that familiar combination of friendship and politics, a wide spectrum of personalities, and the same birthday celebrations, retirement parties and Christmas lunches. Some people will be having a whale of a time and a few will be struggling, but most will be somewhere in between.

Students are the apprentices in the lab. Undergraduate and Masters students will be around for a few months at the most and need a lot of supervision. PhD[14] students stay for three or more years, and develop their own project. Post-doctoral researchers (post-docs for short) have finished and passed their PhDs, and are there to get a few more years' research experience before they can think about setting up their own lab, or joining a commercial research and development company. Others stay at graduate level, working as technicians or lab managers – providing a backbone of vital expertise as students and post-docs come and go.

The most senior scientist in the lab is the principal investigator (PI), lab head or group leader: someone like Harvey McMahon who has established his or her own research group. PIs are recruited by a university or research institute, given some start-up money, an office, and a space in which to do their experiments, and it's up to them to make things happen. If they are employed by a university they will be given a class or two to teach alongside their research. So they write lectures, hire a technician or lab manager, order equipment, recruit students and post-docs, and start work.

If I had decided (and been successful enough) to set up my own lab, then the laboratory space, its equipment, and everyone in it would bear my name. I would have had the odd experience of seeing fridges and expensive machines labelled with brightly coloured tape bearing my name, and hearing people talking about "the Bancewicz lab", or in one institute where I worked, "the Bancewicz's", as if I had just acquired a new family.

Each lab has a system of supervision so everyone has someone more experienced to help them on a daily basis. Every student and post-doc also meets individually with the PI from time to time to explain their data in detail, and discuss where their research might be heading. New ideas are based on information gleaned from academic papers, conferences, and online databases, and the results of their experiments are presented to the world through the same channels.

Scientific research is expensive and slow, so it's essential to share time, ideas, expertise, and materials. To help this to happen, researchers make an effort to build community in the lab and with the wider body of scientists in the field. Academic meetings and presentations are balanced with social events and celebrations. Conferences are a place for learning about new ideas, for meeting people and planning collaborations.

A vital part of the senior scientist's job is to write grant applications. The institute that hired them will pay their salary and some of the lab running costs, but each lab head needs to bring in money to pay for their own research. Every year government bodies, charities, and large companies offer grants for specific types of research, and PIs must come up with bright ideas for new projects, fill in long forms, and wait many months to see whether their applications are successful. The funding process is extremely competitive so getting a new lab started is a challenge, but once the results begin to come the work can build a momentum of its own.

The output of each lab is judged by the quality of the academic journals they publish in, and whether their work makes a lasting contribution to the field. It is also judged by whether they hold any patents, which represent new and useful innovations. If they are successful the PI will have the satisfaction of seeing former post-docs and students set up their own research groups, and will have no trouble recruiting the brightest young minds to take their places.

I have worked in five labs, and they all had their different characteristics, though each was friendly and welcoming. One of the most distinctive things about a lab can be the ways they find to socialize and let off steam. Putting a bunch of creative people together and giving them the freedom to work at their own pace is a great way to foster successful research, and can also produce some unique social traditions.

I did my PhD at an institute where the common room was the hub of all activity. Coffee breaks were a chance to catch up and relax, but also share ideas and ask for help with difficult experiments. New papers, grants, and successful PhD examinations were celebrated there, and the entire institute was always invited. Champagne (or sparkling wine) was served in the traditional way: chilled on ice and sipped from disposable water cooler cups. Christmas parties involved comedy sketches where the students mercilessly ragged the senior staff, and poked fun at any bureaucratic nonsense that had happened the preceding year.

Another lab I worked in ate lunch together every day and took it in turns to bring cake on Friday afternoons. The Christmas "Secret Santa" involved elaborate homemade presents, and at lab celebrations we fired champagne corks down the corridor. When you spend so much time together in a small space, you get to know each other very well.

Eureka!

So what has to happen before the corks can be fired? We might hear the story of a eureka moment when someone realizes, "So that's how it works!" and suddenly a whole area of science changes as everyone rushes to use this new piece of information, but that's not how scientific discoveries usually happen. For most scientists, finding something out is a very gradual process of seeing things coming together.

A discovery in biology often starts with a new PhD student nervously beginning their project. There are long days in the lab, and many false turns, before the first promising data emerges. These results are presented to critical colleagues who suggest further experiments. Others might come on board to help with certain aspects of the project. New experiments are designed, and months are spent testing different ideas. The final pieces of data are generated, and then the student spends long days bent over a hot computer writing a dense and meticulously referenced paper. The paper is submitted to a journal, the anonymous reviewers give some feedback, a few more experiments might need to be done, then resubmission and a long wait. Finally the paper is accepted and the whole research group joins in the celebration.

The above story of the student is only the simplest possible version of events. The process of producing successful research can involve large numbers of people over several years, international collaborations, promising leads that go stale, and surprising results from unexpected places. And everyone has their blind spots: maybe a bias, a pet theory, or a student who botched one of their experiments and failed to confess it.

So in almost every instance of scientific discovery, no single experiment will do, no lab can change the course of history, and no individual can go it alone. Every major development is a painstaking building up of multiple layers of evidence by many people, and each paper and its champagne celebration is just a small milestone along the way. It's very telling that Nobel prizes are usually awarded many years after a discovery is made. The work must be tried and tested thoroughly before anyone can say the course of scientific history has been changed.

What does good science look like?

Harvey McMahon has seen his fair share of celebrations. When I asked him what good science looks like, his replies covered both technique and people management. People do experiments and guide research projects, so to do science well you need to understand human nature. He started by saying that "a student needs to start with experiments that are actually achievable. Progress in science is often limited by what can be done rather than what you feel you should be able to do." I can't help feeling that would be a good principle for life in general.

McMahon works closely with his students to help them develop their experimental technique. "The first result is exciting for the student because they have done something new, so they should enjoy that moment and show off their results to everybody. But experiments are only believable if they can be reproduced, so you get them to do it again two or three times. If the same data keep coming up you take that result apart and figure out all the different reasons why it looks that way."

Some of this interpretation will be interesting and some will be very mundane. One of the questions Harvey asks is, "Is the data significant, or was the equipment not calibrated properly?" The next set of experiments that person designs will include control samples to test for those possibilities, and also several other ways of checking the result. "The second round of results will almost certainly produce a more complete answer," said Harvey, "a small piece of real information about the question they are trying to answer. Eventually what you are hoping for is that each individual will contribute much more than the pieces of information themselves. They will contribute useful knowledge."

Success in science also involves having good intuition. For Harvey, this means "getting the best information and putting it all together in the light of your own experience, constantly questioning what you are doing and making sure the next experiment is not just a random shot in the dark. You need to know the techniques that are more likely to work, and which are most accurate. We now have access to an amazing number of techniques, so you do the experiment first one way and then another." This principle is a bit like doing a sum and then subtracting the numbers afterwards to see if you did it right the first time. The other thing to do is ask questions that might disprove what you've done. Trying to prove yourself wrong is a rigorous way to do science.

When I asked Harvey about "eureka moments", he said that "sometimes new paradigms come about almost imperceptibly. Someone publishes a paper here, then another person does work that agrees or disagrees with it there, and then half a dozen other people say they found it first. You never know when to celebrate, but at some point you need to open the champagne bottle and enjoy your achievement."

Harvey described the first time, about fifteen years ago, when he found evidence that the shape of a cell was determined by proteins embedded in its outer membrane. "Nowadays that seems completely trivial," he explained, "but nobody agreed with me then. So I had arguments with absolutely everybody in the canteen about it." Those conversations helped him to come up with different ways to defend his theory, and determined the course of his work in the lab. "I found people who were willing to do experiments with me, and we got evidence that proteins shape membranes. Nowadays people accept it, but initially it was a hunch that developed very, very slowly."

Questioning

The picture of science I have painted so far is a far cry from what most of us learn at school. As a PhD student in Edinburgh I joined a church that was conveniently located next to a number of good pubs. Some of us used to pile into one of these establishments after the Sunday evening service, and the ensuing conversation ranged from "Who are you?" (it was a big church) to discussions of the sermon we had just heard, and other more philosophical issues.

On one of these Sunday pub nights I sat next to a photography student, and when I introduced myself as a geneticist she said something along the lines of, "All those facts and figures are not for me, I'm an arts student." Rather than just moving on, which would have been infinitely easier, I tried to explain why I thought science was more than a bunch of facts.

We started out by talking about textbooks. No matter how well written a scientific textbook might be or how lavish its illustrations, it is unlikely to make it onto anyone's bedside table except during exam time. I pointed out that textbooks have their place, but the dynamic nature of science means that they're out of date before they're printed.

I explained that the job of scientists (such as McMahon and his lab members) is to go to the shelf of unanswered questions, pick out one they know a bit about and think they can tackle, take it to the lab, and start looking for answers. As they work they'll find things out but they'll also discover more questions, some of which they investigate and some of which are put on the shelf for later. As soon as they begin to make progress they start putting together a scientific paper. After they've published their article, celebrated, and had a bit of sleep, they throw their new paper gleefully over their shoulder and run back to the shelf of unanswered questions. What next? What about that thing that looked weird in the last experiment – is that worth following up? Let's test the theory we just published even further – does it apply in other circumstances? Every stage in the enquiry is a step closer to a truer understanding of the world.

My friend was surprised, and said she would have found science much more exciting if it had been presented that way at school. It's sometimes difficult to get the message across that science is a process and not an encyclopedia, but science teachers need to shout it as loudly as possible before any more young people are duped into thinking that science is boring.

Ignorance

In the real world of science, a certain kind of ignorance drives forward the process of investigation. Harvey McMahon told me how he got a reputation as a talker when he was a post-doc in the USA, and was invited to attend the lab meetings of Michael Brown and Joseph Goldstein. These two men ran an unusual joint lab, collaborated together on cholesterol research, and won a Nobel Prize for their work. Harvey said that "they used to invite me along to their lab meeting simply because I used to always ask questions and they like people to ask questions". In return, he got to learn about some of the best research happening at the time. Clearly the drive to find out "Why?" and "What's that?" is still important to successful science.

Taking this idea even further, a neuroscientist from Columbia University has written a book called *Ignorance: How it Drives Science*.[15] The author, Stuart Firestein, describes how he loved lab science, but found teaching a bit of a struggle. The problem was that he was following the textbook, and had forgotten to highlight the unknown areas or rival theories. He had missed out the most interesting bits.

Firestein's analogy for scientific research is that it's like looking for a black cat in a dark room. "It's groping and probing and poking, and some bumbling and bungling…" Eventually someone finds a light switch, and a solution is revealed. Everyone exclaims, "Oh, wow, so that's how it looks", then they troop into the next dark room. This process is exciting to scientists, so when left to themselves they tend to talk about what is unknown, rather than the contents of books. As Marie Curie said, "One never notices what has been done; one can only see what remains to be done…"[16]

So to counteract his unthinking tendency to teach only the known, Firestein created a new course called *Ignorance*. The quandary is, do you want a good mark or a bad one in Ignorance 101? And would you want to be asked to teach on it? Thankfully, Firestein's colleagues accepted his invitation to present the most puzzling problems in their field, and it was a popular course. This perceptive sort of ignorance leads to good questions and successful research programmes. As Einstein said, "Thoroughly conscious ignorance is the prelude to every real advance in science."[17]

Day science and night science

The day-to-day scientific process of asking questions and looking for answers is as directed as it can be, but as Firestein said, it always involves an element of searching in the dark. François Jacob, a Nobel Prize-winning biologist, described this process as "night science". In his biography, Jacob explained that

> night science ... hesitates, stumbles, recoils, sweats, wakes with a start. Doubting everything, it is forever trying to find itself, question itself, pull itself back together. Night science is a sort of workshop of the possible where what will become the building material of science is worked out ... Where phenomena are still no more than solitary events with no link between them ... Where thought makes its way along meandering paths and twisting lanes, most often leading nowhere ... What guides the mind, then, is not logic but instinct, intuition. The need to understand.[18]

Jacob's description is rather dramatic but it captures the intuitive process that Harvey McMahon described to me: the educated guesses that sometimes work and sometimes don't, and the slow hunch[19] that develops as evidence is gathered together.

Harvey explained that in science, you develop a hypothesis based on what you see in the scientific literature, drawing different threads of knowledge or part-knowledge together. If possible, it's good to test whether the results reported in the papers you read are true. Do the same experiments work in your own lab? You develop a number of hypotheses, and eventually you find one more believable than the others so you start testing it. What follows is not a random process but one that uses a variety of different approaches to test the same idea. Do I see evidence for my hypothesis at a biochemical level, in cells, or in patients? There will be failures, but because you are working at a number of different levels you should develop a fuller understanding of the phenomenon you're trying to study.

After going round and round questioning things, testing and trying, you finally have something to say: some new knowledge about the world. That's when "day science" starts. You gather all the data together and line it up in a sensible order so you can explain what it is that you found. Everything is clear. Details about the day the freezer broke, your computer crashed, or when you couldn't start an experiment because the chemical you needed was missing are now irrelevant.

A scientist knows that night science has to happen before a nice clear paper can be written, but another reader might think lab work is as straightforward as following a recipe. As Jacob said:

> Day science employs reasoning that meshes
> like gears, and achieves results with the force of
> certainty. One admires its majestic arrangement as
> that of a da Vinci painting or a Bach fugue. One
> walks about in it as in a formal French garden.
> Conscious of its progress, proud of its past, sure of
> its future, day science advances in light and glory.[20]

The separation between day and night science is useful for the scientist. No journal wants to print details about how your friend in Australia emailed you advice every day until you managed to get a certain piece of equipment working, or that you took a long time to finish your experiments because you had a heavy teaching load that term. That information wouldn't help another researcher to understand your experiments, but on the other hand, it shouldn't be hidden away completely. Biographies like Jacob's are a valuable reminder that science is an exciting process carried out by real people.

A very, very short introduction to the philosophy of science

There are other ways of thinking about how science works, and these come from the philosophy of science. Philosophers are very good at scrutinizing the assumptions that scientists make, and checking whether what they say matches up with what they do. The sorts of questions they ask are, "What are the limits of science?", "What sorts of questions can it can answer successfully?" and "What separates science from non-science?"

On exploring the philosophy of science I quickly discovered that I was not going to get any easy answers. Philosophers love disagreeing with one another, and scientists do not always agree with what philosophers say. I suspect this disconnect happens partly because scientists and philosophers speak different languages, and inhabit different cultures. Nevertheless, some of the insights of philosophy are very helpful for understanding the everyday practice of science.

The first is that science is different to mathematics. You can prove things mathematically, deducing an answer from general principles. So if even numbers are divisible by two, six is definitely an even number. Science, on the other hand, is inductive: experimentalists examine evidence and come up with (or induce) general principles, which are not expressed as certainties, but as probabilities. If all known cows are ruminants and I find an animal that looks like a cow, it is probably going to be a ruminant.

Scientists move from limited data (an examination of cows in a part of the world) to a more general conclusion (all cows are ruminants). Probabilities are never definite, so these sorts of investigations give provisional conclusions. One day we might find a species that shares all the characteristics of cows, but which has one stomach not four, and we will need to come up with some new categories.

Night science is often messier than simple induction,[21] but the principle of induction is still important. Harvey McMahon described how the inductive process works in his own area of neurobiology. Often the papers that are published contain errors – not deliberately, but because that was the understanding at the time. He explained that "the experiments you have done are still fine. If someone else tries to come along and reproduce it they are able to do that. It's just that the interpretation – the line of logical thinking that you have drawn through the data – is not actually quite right." Later on you might find a better way to interpret the data, so you do some more experiments based on your new idea and publish another paper.

Someone in another lab may read your first paper and

think you're wrong, so they try to repeat your work and come up with a different hypothesis. Harvey is always pleased when people do this because it refines his work and shows what is important and what needs redoing. He said, "It's much more interesting when people are actually trying to disprove you and say that you are wrong, and testing your hypothesis for you." You have to be pretty secure to take that sort of criticism, but if your motivation is primarily to discover the truth about the world, you have to learn to be part of a wider conversation than just the one happening in your lab.

Over the centuries, the inductive approach has turned out to be a very successful way of predicting things about the world. When new discoveries are confirmed, we can use them to develop new technologies. Planes, computers, medicines, and buildings are all evidence of the high level of trust we place in science.

Another useful approach in science is inference to the best explanation. This is detective work: a) water absorbs and emits light of a certain frequency; b) we observe that same frequency of light coming from a planet far away; c) so the planet has water on its surface. The next step is to test that inference with some further experiments. In the end, you make a case for your hypothesis using all the evidence you have found and your colleagues judge whether or not you have made a good case. The best way to show confidence in another person's work is to base your own research on it. You'll soon find out whether they did their experiments well or not.

After induction and "inference to the best explanation", things start to get more complicated and some people begin to get dissatisfied with philosophy of science at this stage. Experimental scientists are practical people, and they use modes of enquiry that work. Of course it's good to examine your assumptions and biases, but when it comes to deciding whether the physical world exists outside of human thought, things start to get a bit too abstract for many people. As Samir Okasha writes in his book *Philosophy of Science: A Very Short Introduction*, from time to time philosophers of science have tried to tell scientists what is and isn't possible – and were often wrong.

In the end, defining science is extremely difficult because the techniques of different fields are so varied. Astronomy is a historical science because light from distant galaxies takes billions of years to get here. Geology and evolutionary biology also involve historical detective work. Theoretical physicists find that mathematics can be used to model reality so effectively that they sometimes rely on equations in the face of apparent hard evidence, assuming that the experimentalists will eventually discover their theory is correct. Experimentalists, on the other hand, want to see the hard evidence before they accept a theory.

Most scientists are reductionists, breaking things down to their constituent bits and pieces, but every field has its limits. Most biologists work with organisms, cells, and tissues, or collections of molecules, while chemists are more interested in the molecules themselves, or in atoms.[22] Physicists go even further and break down the atoms. Ecologists and others like them are anti-reductionists, working on groups of organisms across large areas. Any attempt at a precise definition of science always leaves something out or includes an academic field that traditionally has nothing to do with science, such as history or literature.

In general, science usually ticks most of the following boxes.[23]

1. It is the study of objects or phenomena that can be weighed, measured or observed.
2. Questions of meaning or value are excluded.
3. It uses generalizations about properties or mathematical descriptions of them.
4. Scientific statements are always provisional, and open to falsification.
5. Personal bias is reduced to a minimum, with layers of accountability and repetition by others to reduce bias even further.

This is the most common approach by scientists, and is known as critical realism. Critical realists believe there is definitely a physical world out there that we can study, but that our knowledge is neither exhaustive nor final.[24]

Motivations

As well as being realists, scientists are also human. They are attracted to science for a variety of reasons, though inspiring and supportive family or teachers nearly always play a large part in developing their curiosity about the natural world. Their motivations for sticking with science as a career after university, despite all the demands and uncertainties that such a life brings, are equally varied and at times surprising.

Some of the main drivers for science are fascination or curiosity, the enjoyment of meeting a challenge, the privilege of making discoveries, the prospect of new technologies further down the line, and perhaps ambition to make a name for oneself. There is also the immense satisfaction when things come together and begin to make sense. So far, so predictable. More unexpected drivers are the enjoyable process of tinkering with experimental systems, and the opportunity to exercise creativity and imagination.

For Harvey McMahon, his interest is in how things work. Of course he wants to understand disease processes, but when you operate at the level of molecules you need to focus on smaller details. There is also pride in good craftsmanship. At a day-to-day level, neurobiology is often very mundane: cutting and pasting DNA, making solutions and growing cells or bacteria – and Harvey loves all that. On some days your main achievement is to have followed the recipe or method correctly, not being too hasty and spoiling it, or getting distracted and missing out a step. The long-term goal is what other people are interested in, so you have to be very self-motivated and enjoy your work in order to get through enough routine days before you can find out something significant. As Harvey said, "You have to be interested in every individual step; it's not just the final result that you are interested in."

The rewards for doing science range from the utilitarian – solving problems or gaining useful knowledge – to the spiritual. As I mentioned in chapter one, some professional scientists have experiences that are compatible with but different to scientific descriptions: that feeling of pure joy when you find yourself discovering something for the first time; delight in the beauty of nature or scientific data; the ideals or ethical standards we set for ourselves; or the importance we place on certain relationships. For a person of faith, there is the added pleasure of knowing that you are studying the creator's work.

Relating science and religion

The real world of science is a million miles away from the debates on science and religion that happen from time to time in the media. Perhaps scientists are all a little crazy (who would put in the hours otherwise), but they're definitely not identical in other ways. Behind every piece of research is a team of people representing different faiths and belief systems.

The careful scrutiny of data is central to science, so although someone's worldview will no doubt inform their behaviour or the research subject they choose, it is easy enough for people of different faith backgrounds to work together in the lab. Worldview is more influential in the humanities or social sciences, and in my interactions with academics and students I have realized that those subjects are more challenging for people of diverse views – though I expect, as in science, coming at the same subject from a variety of different angles is hugely beneficial. We all have blind spots.

Harvey is a Christian because he saw that type of faith lived out around him as a child. He counts himself fortunate to have had good role models in the family he was brought up in. He believed in God from very early on, and found the way his Christian relatives lived very attractive. Of course it's very difficult to live a consistent life, and we are not perfect people. Harvey certainly saw that in his family, but at least they understood their failings, and there were no double standards. He simply wanted to be like these people, rather than copying his friends at school.

When he is working, Harvey experiences the awe and wonder that many scientists talk about. He also feels that God is with him in his work. He said, "I believe God is genuinely interested in me, and that when I do my work I am reflecting something of what he has allowed me to do. That's not just a passive process, it's something he has permitted me to discover, but he has also shown me something. People often ask me, 'How on earth do you end up with such high productivity from such a small lab?' I will reply that I believe God has allowed that to happen – it's not just by chance. The things we have worked on are actually something God delights in, and delights to show people. At the end of the day, it's quite a religious experience doing science."

Chapter 3

Christianity and Science

We must find the right thread on which to string the pearls of our observations, so that they disclose their true pattern.

William Whewell, scientist & philosopher[25]

... his religion was not ... a theory but ... a love affair.
Gilbert K. Chesterton, writer & critic[26]

I am often asked what it is like to be a Christian in science. After reading the last chapter, hopefully it's easier to see that science is way of investigating the world that is entirely compatible with faith. The real challenge is to explain what I believe in the context of a society where the consensus seems to be that God either doesn't exist, or doesn't care. Most people keep quiet about religion – perhaps because it's too personal and they don't want to offend anyone, or they want to avoid an argument, or they just don't have time. I found that my own conversations about faith in the lab were as awkward or easy as they are in any other place of work.

Over the last ten years, I have interviewed a number of senior scientists who are also Christians. For most of them there came a point when they had the opportunity to make their beliefs known in a very public way, either through advertising a faith-based event on the staff email list, accepting an invitation to speak for a Christian group on campus, or simply allowing the clutter of their personal (i.e. Christian) life to invade their office. The reactions among their students and colleagues were varied, and often surprising.

None of these scientists has ever expressed any regret at being open about their beliefs. Their relationships with their colleagues are now more meaningful than if they had kept quiet, and their students have learned that science and faith are not opposites – something I found helpful myself at the same stage. When I was an undergraduate at Aberdeen University, I was a member of the same church as a professor from the physics department. As I explored my own beliefs and figured out how they fitted with my studies, it was encouraging to see the evidence every Sunday that science is not against faith.

Many readers will already know Christianity from the inside. For those who do not, I will briefly explain why I have chosen to be a Christian. I will also describe why I think my faith is compatible with science. This is not intended to be a comprehensive summary – I am not a theologian or a philosopher of science. Its purpose is simply to show a little of my heart, and also challenge some of the most common preconceived ideas about both science and Christianity. I have deliberately kept this chapter short because I want to spend most of my time focusing on the ways in which science enhances faith. For those who would like more in-depth explanations, I have recommended some books and articles that take things further.

Why am I a Christian?

One of the best analogies for an examination of Christianity is a legal trial. In any court, the evidence is gathered, debated, and examined from different viewpoints. Before a judgment can be made, the evidence must be shown to be reliable. W. K. Clifford, a nineteenth-century mathematician and philosopher, said, "it is wrong always, everywhere, and for everyone, to believe anything on insufficient evidence".[27] Clifford was an atheist, but I agree with him. My faith affects how I live my life, so I want to know I'm not trusting in fairy tales.

In the case for God, there are different categories of evidence. We are often encouraged to trust science above almost every other type of knowledge, but some questions are outside the scope of science. At the most basic level, the scientific enterprise itself rests on a number of assumptions that come from outside science. We take it for granted that we are rational, that the world is worth exploring, that experiments are repeatable, and that we can expect to find law-like behaviour in the universe. There is also the idea that we can describe things logically and mathematically. These assumptions work, but you can't prove them scientifically[28] – they could even be described as steps of faith.

There are other ways of thinking that aren't scientific, but they are just as important. Poetry uses language that is neither precise nor scientific, but it expresses truth very powerfully. For anyone who has ever experienced winter, the line from John Keats, "Ah, bitter chill it was! The owl, for all his feathers was a-cold", will be enough to get them reaching for another layer. I could give a precise scientific description of cold weather and the biological reasons why it might feel unpleasant to feel cold, but it would take a lot longer and be far less memorable than Keats's version. For everyday life, metaphor is often more useful than mechanism.[29]

In the end, science can tell us with great accuracy how the material world works, but it cannot answer questions about ultimate truth, meaning or values. Who shall I vote for? Should we invade Iraq? Is that painting beautiful? As the Astronomer Royal Martin Rees said, "I think just as religion is separate from science, so is ethics … There are lots of important things that are separate from science."[30] Science can tell us how things are, but it cannot tell us how things ought to be: for that, we need other types of knowledge.

Christians believe in a personal God, so the analogy of a human relationship is also useful here. If you enter into any sort of romance, science will establish if the object of your affections is *homo sapiens*, but beyond that it's not much help. You will no doubt weigh up other kinds of evidence: information about that person, personal experience, past history, a weighing of probable outcomes, and the advice of others. You might also need to take a bit of a risk. If the person is really who they seem to be, the risk should pay off.

Three types of evidence, both scientific and non-, have been important to me in my own examination of Christianity. First, there is both great beauty and a fantastic level of order in the universe. To me, these are hints that suggest an organizing mind or being was involved in its origins. The fact that we can make sense of the world using mathematics is astounding. Could a chaotic, uncontrolled process have produced a world that can be understood in this way? It also looks as if the universe was set up so that life could evolve: an argument called "fine-tuning" or "the anthropic principle".

I am cautious about relying too much on scientific evidence for God, and I will explain my reasons in chapter six. I tend to hold on to the fine-tuning and beauty arguments very lightly, seeing them more as supporting data than conclusive evidence. The scientific picture sets the scene for a more in-depth examination of who God is.

The second set of evidence that's important to me is the Bible and the history of the church. If you stop at fine-tuning you end up with deism: the idea that God is there but we have no interaction with him, her, or it. But I was drawn to a God who revealed himself in person. Christians believe that God created the universe and everything in it. The first chapter of Genesis describes how God made us "in his own image" (Genesis 1:26–27), and gave us a special responsibility to look after the world. He chose a specific group of people, the Israelites, and built a relationship with them. After working through that one nation, God finally came to show himself to everyone.

God is Father, Son, and Holy Spirit: three persons in one. The most accessible information about God can be found by looking at the person of Jesus, God's Son in human form. He was born into a poor family, the son of a carpenter, and remained poor throughout his life. By his actions he showed that God is wise, loving, and forgiving, respects people regardless of their gender, age, race, or position in society, and hates injustice and religious hypocrisy. Jesus travelled around Israel, inviting people to know God and live life to the full.

He taught by asking questions and telling challenging stories, always making people think more than they really wanted to. Rules are easy, but keeping to the spirit of the law involves thoughtful engagement in every situation.

The Christian way of living involves a level of generosity, forgiveness, and love that is difficult to sustain. Instead of leaving us to die and be separated from God, which is the natural consequence of our wrongdoing, Jesus died in our place. After Jesus came back to life (there was no way God was going to stay dead) and returned to his Father, his followers carried on his work, helped by the Holy Spirit. The church was born: not a building, but a group of people who worship God and try to follow Jesus' teaching, supporting each other and reaching out to the community around them.

The events recorded in the Bible are supported by historical evidence. The vast majority of historians agree that Jesus of Nazareth existed, was an itinerant teacher or Rabbi, developed a large following, and was executed by the Romans. He was buried in a guarded tomb but his body vanished, and many of his disciples died for their claim that he is alive. Jesus' following increased dramatically, Christians became famous for being a positive force in society, and the church has never stopped growing since.

Today, the church is worldwide, incredibly diverse, and still following Jesus' teaching. Of course people are not perfect, and Christians are not God's puppets, so we mess things up – that's the whole point: why else would we need Jesus? Despite our limitations, the church remains God's way of working in the world. We can't function well alone. In the end Jesus promised to come again and renew everything – so if we suffer now, that is not the way things will always be.

The third piece of important evidence for God is the effect he has on individual lives. I learned about God as a child, and as I grew, my understanding of him grew. I knew my parents would love me whatever I chose to believe, but once I understood more about Jesus I decided to be a Christian. Later on, as an older teenager, I had a period when I wondered whether I just believed in God because my parents believed in him. I was studying philosophy at school, and that made me think about the claims of Christianity in more depth. In the end, the most important line of evidence for me was answered prayers and changed lives. When someone you know well becomes a Christian you have the opportunity to see whether Jesus' claims are really true. I've seen this change in someone's life happen over and over again, including my own.

Science and Christianity

After the legal trial or relationship approaches, another way to explore Christianity is as a thought experiment. If a powerful and loving God existed, what would you expect? This was the approach of the scholar and writer C. S. Lewis, who said, "I believe in Christianity as I believe that the sun has risen not only because I see it but because by it I see everything else."[31] The claims of Christianity are consistent with what we see in the world. They make sense of both science and human nature. The evidence may be open to alternative conclusions, so we have to decide which makes best sense of the data.[32]

Many scientists have taken this approach to Christianity.

Several of the people I interviewed for the *Test of FAITH* book had been challenged to look at the evidence for God by a friend. They realized that until that point they had not investigated it properly, and were courageous enough to start looking with an open mind. One of the marks of excellence in science is to be aware that you might be wrong and be prepared to think again, even if it means changing the whole direction of your future research.

For a scientist, the concept of truth is something real and solid – a brute fact that you can't deny. If you discover the truth that's a good thing; that's the whole point of life, even if the consequences are a bit uncomfortable to begin with, and others might think you're crazy. If the data (either scientific or other kinds of evidence) and your interpretation of it were good, then that risk will be worth it.

For a scientist who *is* a Christian, how does their faith affect their work, and vice versa? There are inevitably some issues to consider but, on the whole, science is a natural home for a Christian. A recent survey of scientists in the US found that 61 per cent identified themselves as Christians, compared with nearly 74 per cent in the general population. Considering the aggressive nature of the science-faith debate in the US, those figures are extremely encouraging – large numbers of Christians are still studying science.[33] Statistics are not available for the UK, but as the discussion is less polarized, I suspect the proportion of Christians in science would be even closer to the number in the general population.

These figures show that science and faith are compatible, but a closer investigation shows that they are more than that: they are also complementary. Science can help faith to flourish, and faith can feed into science in helpful ways. We might get the opposite impression from the media, but historians have begun to recognize that religion played a positive role in the development of science. Noah Efron of Bar-Ilan University has written that "one cannot recount the history of modern science without acknowledging the crucial importance of Christianity".[34]

Modern science has its roots in ancient Greek philosophy, which used geometry and other forms of mathematics. Scholars in India, Egypt, and Persia also developed ways of thinking that contributed to the development of science. Texts from all of these countries made their way – alongside Chinese technology – to the Islamic world in the Middle Ages, and Islamic scholars made progress in philosophy, mathematics, astronomy, and medicine.[35] From the twelfth century onwards, Arabic and Greek texts began to make their way to Europe, were translated into Latin, and European scholars started to do "natural philosophy".

As this new wave of ancient learning was absorbed and modified by Christian thinkers in Europe, science began to emerge in a form that we would recognize today. The mathematics that the Greek philosopher Plato taught was incredibly important for the growth of the physical sciences, but lacked an emphasis on experimentation. The early natural philosophers (as scientists were called until the nineteenth century) reasoned that because God wasn't limited by anything when he created, it would be impossible to predict what things were like unless you studied them first. For Isaac Newton, Robert Boyle, and others like them, scientific experiments became a key to exploring God's creation.

Another example of how theology influenced scientific thinking is in the concept of scientific laws. The idea of rules that describe the movement of objects, chemical processes, and so on, came initially from the biblical idea of a God who creates everything in an orderly way. The Old Testament in particular has a strong emphasis on God sustaining the world in regular ways: day and night, cycles of the moon, birth and death, winter and summer. So the pioneering early scientists expected to find law-like behaviour in the world, and this step of faith was well rewarded. We now know that matter behaves in regular ways that can be described by laws and physical constants, which we can use to make predictions and develop technologies.

Of course, there have been occasional conflicts between science and the church, though remarkably few, and perhaps only one has had any significant impact. In the seventeenth century, leaders in the Roman Catholic Church felt it their duty to make sure scientists toed a particular line, and the infamous Galileo incident is probably the most well-known of these. There is a certain amount of mythology surrounding this incident, so it's worth spending some time looking at what really happened.

The science of Galileo's day said that all the planets orbit earth, and this was thought to match the latest interpretation of the Bible. Galileo found evidence that supported a sun-centred model, an alternative that had been proposed by the astronomer Copernicus a few decades earlier. He began to publicize his views, saying that we should not get science from the Bible. Some Jesuit priests came to Galileo and told him that the earth couldn't move because the Bible says in Psalm

93 that "the world is established; it shall never be moved".[36] Galileo pointed out that such poetic passages from the Bible are hymns of praise to be sung in the Temple, not scientific texts.

Although Galileo was right about biblical interpretation, and his contribution to experimental science was phenomenal, there was no overwhelming evidence in his day that the earth orbits the sun. His scientific publications were tolerated until he insulted the Pope and incited the wrath of the inquisition. The Roman Catholic Church was particularly twitchy at this time because the Reformation was underway and large numbers of people were breaking away to form a new denomination. The response of the Vatican was to crack down on heresy, including suppression of the sun-centred universe theory.

After a run-in with the church authorities, Galileo was put under house arrest for the rest of his life, where he continued to do science in comfortable (although restricted) circumstances. The Roman Catholic Church has since returned to a more thoughtful interpretation of the Bible, and apologized wholeheartedly for what was done to Galileo. Overall the church as a whole has been supportive of science, and the majority of the early modern scientists were Christians.

There is one other significant exception to the picture of harmony between science and faith. In recent years, some Christians have started to interpret the Bible as if it contains scientific as well as theological truth. This movement began with the Seventh-day Adventists in the US back in the 1920s, became popular among other Christian denominations in the 1960s and seventies, and has now spread around the globe. This view is called Young Earth Creationism, because if you work through the Bible from the six days described in Genesis to the birth of Jesus, counting the years given in the genealogies as you go, it looks as if the universe is only 6,000 years old.

The Young Earth view makes it difficult to be involved in any form of science, especially astronomy and evolutionary biology, but it is by no means universal among Christians. It's more common in the US than Europe, and even then it's not as widespread as some think. In a survey of 743 Protestant pastors by the American organization BioLogos in 2012, 19 per cent were fully committed to Young Earth Creationism.[37] That number is significant, but is nowhere near the level that most school pupils expect when they ask me, "How can you believe in both Genesis and evolution?" or "Do you think there was a Big Bang?" Christians believe that God is the creator, but the "how" of creation is a secondary issue.

I believe that the Bible is true and inspired by God. It is also a very ancient text that must be translated and interpreted. We need to understand the historical and cultural context of the writers before anyone can say what it means. Genesis is a prescientific account of creation that describes who God is and why he created the universe, addressing questions of purpose and meaning. What it doesn't do is tell exactly how the universe was created. The phrase "from the dust" in Genesis 2, about the creation of humans, is particularly enigmatic. The biblical account of creation is compatible with the idea that God created slowly, using the processes that astronomy and evolutionary biology reveal to us.

I realize that some Christians disagree with this view, but I hope our differences will not distract from the content of this book. We can all appreciate the beauty and wonder of the world, whatever we believe about the interpretation of Genesis. The Bible describes how God made a good world, and science simply is a way of understanding that world and learning to use its resources wisely. When I connect what I believe about Jesus with what I know about the stars and planets, I am filled with awe. I can speak every day with the one who is in charge of the universe.

When I talk to Christians who work as scientists, they tend to focus on the fact that their work helps them to worship. One well-known Christian in science is Dr Francis Collins, the director of the US National Institutes of Health and former director of the Human Genome Project. In his book *The Language of God*, he speaks for all of these people when he says that it is "possible for the scientist-believer to be intellectually fulfilled and spiritually alive, both worshipping God and using the tools of science to uncover some of the awesome mysteries of his creation".

Various people have proposed models for how science relates to faith, and my own is a Venn diagram: a graphing method my PhD supervisor liked to use for thinking about scientific data. Christianity is the foundation for everything I believe, so that is a big circle that takes up all the available space. Inside that circle are the various activities of life: relationships, work, home, and all the other things that are important to me.

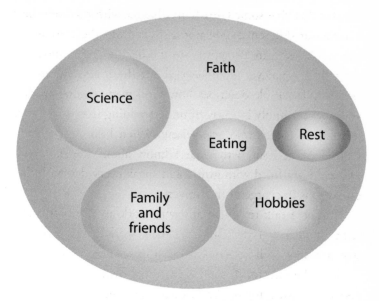

The relationship between my science and faith[38]

Science is one of the activities that happen within the circle of my faith, and it is bounded by its own smaller circle of methods and assumptions. The background of belief is still there, but some things are excluded from scientific practice. For example, I might pray for a colleague's health, or that I would do an experiment well, but I definitely wouldn't pray for a certain result: that wouldn't make any sense if I was trying to find out how the world actually works. Neither would I include poems in a paper. I like poetry, but words are limited in scientific journals and they need to be saved for describing data.

The boundaries around science go both ways. In the same way that certain activities are excluded from experiments, a scientist will leave some attitudes behind when they go home at night. We don't analyse our relationships scientifically, or at least not if they're to remain healthy. And being fascinated by a rare form of cancer is appropriate in the lab, but not at the bedside of a friend or relative. The explanation that studying cancer helps us to understand the way normal cells work will be of little comfort to a person undergoing radiotherapy. Science and faith overlap, but there are some ways of thinking and acting that are appropriate only to science or faith specifically. The benefit of this approach is that anyone can do science, regardless of his or her beliefs, and I think that is a very good thing. We should all be able to enjoy the amazing things science reveals about the world we live in.

Continuing the conversation

My focus for the rest of this book has been to find scientists who are also Christians, and ask them how they see their research and their faith working together. My question was, "How do you start the conversation when someone asks how your faith and science interact?" Most of the people I spoke to wanted to explain their research, why they thought it was exciting, and how that enhanced their experience of God. Creativity, imagination, beauty, wonder, and awe were topics that came spontaneously out of those conversations.

For me, the best part of working in a lab was being able to understand a little of the complexity and interconnectedness of the living world. After a year or so of my PhD studies I realized what a challenge I had taken on, and I wondered whether I would ever be able to produce any meaningful results. This is a humbling process that every new researcher goes through as they come up against the boundaries of the known. Living things are extremely complicated, so you have to choose only a tiny part of an organism to study: maybe a single gene or one feature of its behaviour. It can take years to understand a single aspect of that tiny part in enough depth to be able to publish an academic paper about it. In the end that realization can be exciting, because there is so much more to discover.

Experienced scientists sometimes say that all of human knowledge is insignificant in comparison to what is still unknown, and I can now appreciate that statement. I can also appreciate how enjoyable it is to survey all that un-knowledge, grab a bit, and try to figure it out. I have a better understanding of how vast and intricate the natural world is – my horizons have been expanded, and so has my understanding of God. Appreciating the grandeur of the universe seems to be a universal for humankind, and that is a perfect starting point for discussions about science and faith.

Further reading

Denis Alexander, *Creation or Evolution: Do We Have to Choose?* (Oxford: Monarch, 2014)

Darrel Falk, *Coming to Peace with Science: Bridging the Worlds Between Faith and Biology* (Downers Grove, IL: InterVarsity Press, 2004)

James Hannam, *God's Philosophers: How the Medieval World Laid the Foundations for Modern Science* (London: Icon Books, 2010)

Rodney Holder, *Big Bang, Big God* (Oxford: Lion, 2013)

Tim Keller, *The Reason for God* (New York: Dutton, 2008; London: Hodder & Stoughton, 2009)

C. S. Lewis, *Mere Christianity* (1952. Latest edition, William Collins, 2012)

Ernest Lucas, *Can We Believe Genesis Today?* (Leicester: InterVarsity Press, 2005)

Frank Morison, *Who Moved the Stone?* (1930) https://archive.org/details/WhoMovedTheStone

Ronald Numbers, *Galileo Goes to Jail and Other Myths About Science and Religion* (Harvard University Press, 2010)

Amy Orr-Ewing, *Why Trust the Bible?* (Leicester: InterVarsity Press, 2008)

John Stott, *Basic Christianity* (Leicester: InterVarsity Press, 2008)

The Faraday Papers. A series of short articles on science-faith issues by experienced authors, including John Polkinghorne, Rodney Holder, Denis Alexander and Alister McGrath. (www.faraday-institute.org)

Test of FAITH online briefing sheets and articles (www.testoffaith.com)

Chapter 4

Creativity

The successful scientist thinks like a poet
but works like a bookkeeper.

E. O. Wilson, biologist[39]

... every Christian has his own creative work to do,
his own part in the mystery of the "new creation".

Thomas Merton, writer & Trappist monk[40]

I came to appreciate the creativity of science while studying genetics. Creative people generate ideas and make new things, and I discovered that any lab-based research involves both of those activities in large quantities. One of my favourite courses at university was molecular biology: the study of DNA and proteins. Exploring this micro-world involved problem solving, lateral thinking,[41] and visual model-making, all of which I enjoyed immensely. I also appreciated that fact that we were learning about solutions to real-life issues.

Most things in molecular biology happen in little plastic tubes. First, minuscule quantities of frighteningly expensive colourless liquids are added together using very accurate pipettes. Some of these solutions might smell bad (though you shouldn't really get close enough to find out) and some are unstable at room temperature, so an ice bucket is an essential part of your equipment. Cycles of heating or cooling are often involved, and perhaps the addition of further tiny quantities of clear liquids.

This sort of biology feels a little like magic because the important ingredients – the DNA and proteins – are completely invisible most of the time. In the end, you need to know how to find out what has happened in your plastic tubes. The most usual method is similar to the chromatography you did in school science lessons, but using toxic chemicals and high voltage electricity. The results are then dramatically revealed, either on a computer monitor or in a darkroom.

If the process I have described sounds laborious, that's because it is. It can take weeks to get an experiment running at all, and the patient tinkering involved is an important aspect of scientific creativity. Most of my colleagues in the lab enjoyed playing around with experimental systems, trying to get them to work. If you know what you're looking for, even the most laborious troubleshooting can be very exciting in the end.

The creativity of molecular biology

Let me explain a little of the magic. DNA is a polymer – a long molecule made of thousands of small subunits joined together in a long chain. There are four kinds of subunits in DNA: Adenine (A), Thymine (T), Cytosine (C) and Guanine (G). Two chains of DNA, side by side, make the ladder-like structure of the DNA double helix, with weak chemical bonds as the rungs. Each rung connects an A with a T, or a C with a G – no other pairing is allowed. So if you have the sequence of one side of the ladder you can predict the other.

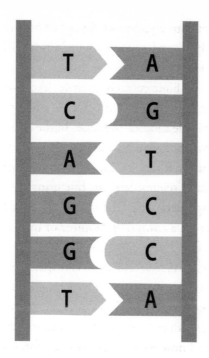

A short section of DNA

The beauty of the DNA ladder is that the rungs (the weak chemical bonds) can be easily broken to split it down the middle lengthways. Each side of the ladder can have a new side built onto it and the result is two DNA ladders, each half old and half new. That's how DNA is replicated in cells, though many other specialized molecules are needed to make the process happen.

The other thing you can do when the ladder splits is to access the information it contains. The four DNA subunits, A, T, C, and G, spell out a code. Sections of this code – the genes – are read off by the machinery of the cell, acting as blueprints for building proteins. So for example, CTCGAGGGGC spells out the beginning of the insulin protein and ACTCTTCTGG codes for part of the haemoglobin molecule, which carries the oxygen inside red blood cells.

The structure of DNA is what makes the art of molecular biology possible. The basic tools of the trade (the aforementioned frighteningly expensive colourless liquids) include solutions of A, T, C, and G, and a selection of enzymes. Enzymes are proteins that help specific chemical reactions to happen, such as digesting other proteins, cutting DNA or making a new DNA chain. With these and a number of other cellular ingredients, you can snip DNA at specific points, extract the sections you need, join them together, make copies, and introduce mutations. Often isolating a whole gene is very complicated[42] so it's a work of real craftsmanship to identify the right parts, isolate them in a series of sections, and reassemble them in a new and useful location.

The true artists of molecular biology are the organisms themselves: the bacteria and viruses that use their tiny genomes to the max. I still remember hearing a lecture about viruses that read some parts of their DNA in all three "open reading frames".[43] That will mean nothing to most readers, but just imagine that in order to solve a paper crisis a resourceful author decides to write a book that contains three separate stories. Each page of the book contains a long stream of letters with no spaces in between. The first story begins with the first letter on the first page, and the beginning of each new word is marked with a dot above the first letter of the word. The second story also begins on page one, a few lines down from the start of the first story. The beginning of each word is marked with an asterisk, and the words overlap with – but are completely different to – the words of the first story. The third story begins a little further on, marked with a different icon.

An embedded series of stories like this would be frustrating to read, and virtually impossible to write, but the book would certainly use less paper! We now know that human DNA also includes some overlapping genes,[44] but overall our genome[45] appears to be much less condensed than that of viruses.

The story of the resourceful virus had me captivated. I was impressed that something as small as a virus could use its DNA in such a powerful way. Molecular biologists get ideas from organisms like this, borrow their cellular tools, and are able to study the natural world at a level of detail that was undreamt of fifty years ago.

So scientific creativity is different from artistic creativity because it is often hidden. Scientific output itself is not an art form, though the data can be beautiful. To return to the metaphor of chapter two, the most creative part of science is night science – putting different pieces of information together, having innovative ideas, problem solving, and making experimental systems that work – all of which usually happens away from the public eye. What most of us get to hear is day science: the clean-cut solution to a problem, but not the creative process of arriving at that solution.

Exploring creativity

I became so convinced that creativity is important in science that when I was interviewed for a Masters course at Edinburgh University I mentioned it (ever so modestly) as my own best quality, and something that suited me for science. I was then humbled as I started my first long-term lab project and realized what scientific creativity actually involves. Precise experimental technique, patience, careful observation, resourcefulness, and experience are just as important as bright ideas. E. O. Wilson is right: science is a mixture of poetry and accounting.

Both this and the next chapter are about the process of doing science. Creativity and imagination are essential ingredients in everyday research, and they are also important to people of faith. Why do we value creativity so highly? Where does creativity come from? There is a wealth of thinking on this subject in both science and theology.

For many scientists who are also Christians, their faith grows as they learn to use their creative gifts in the lab. And not only does science enhance faith, for these people faith can also enhance science. Christianity is about living life to the full, and for a believing scientist their faith gives them a framework for doing what they do to the best of their ability. My hope is that when we understand these motivations, it will help us to have a more fruitful conversation about science and faith.

Creativity came up in a number of my conversations with scientists at the start of this project, and also in a survey of European researchers, where creativity was named as one of the values that was most important to them.[46] I approached Dr Ruth Hogg, a vision scientist from Northern Ireland, to find out what she thought about creativity in science and her own Christian faith. I had already met Ruth when she was living in Cambridge, working at a post-doc in the Vision

Laboratory at the University of Cambridge. She had trained as an optometrist, and decided to focus on research rather than purely clinical work. After a PhD in Belfast, a couple of years of post-doctoral research in Melbourne, and a stint at Cambridge, she moved back to Northern Ireland to lecture and run her own research group at Queen's University, Belfast.

Ruth works on age-related macular degeneration, which is the biggest cause of blindness in the older generation. The macula is the most sensitive part of the eye and is responsible for most of our vision, especially detailed work like reading. Work on this disease is urgently needed because, as Ruth explained, "There have been treatments developed in the last five years that have advanced things slightly, but it still has a big impact on people's quality of life. There's still a lot to do." She and her colleagues are looking at the different factors that affect whether a person will develop macular degeneration later in life, and particularly those that are inherited.

Ruth is a very creative person, and the first thing I discovered on talking to her is that she is an accomplished pianist. In her mid teens she wanted to be a musician, but she eventually settled on science instead. Ruth's perspective is coloured by this early experience. "I guess I've always been able to see the creativity required to do science. Anybody who has done classical training knows that although there is creativity within music, there's also a very strict structure that we all need to work within. We need to understand harmony and theory, and so on. It's really only through understanding that theory that you can learn to take your music to a different level."

Ruth has found that science, like music, involves both learning and inspiration. "There's a method that we're all working within, but to do something new and exciting you really do need the creativity." Even the entry requirement into the world of science requires creativity. She reminded me that "the basic criterion for a PhD is to produce something novel within your field".

To be creative in science, said Ruth, "you've got to know where the field is going, and how you can contribute to it. There are only limited sources of funding, so you have to be innovative in finding things to apply for. That in itself can be a good thing, because it broadens your horizons, and makes you think a bit more widely. Teaching students requires a kind of creativity as well." Ruth had a number of other interesting insights about creativity in science and faith, so I will return to her story at various points throughout this chapter.

The roots of creativity

Creativity could be defined as the "ability to bring about the new and valuable": value being measured by truth, goodness, beauty or usefulness.[47] I thought the concept of creativity would have its roots in biblical language, but I was wrong. God created and we are God's creation, but the word "creativity" doesn't appear at all in either the Old or New Testaments. God creates, but obviously nobody felt they needed a special word to describe that aspect of God's character. The concept of human creativity was also a relative latecomer.[48] The idea that we might mirror God's act of creation in any way was considered blasphemous for a long time.[49]

People began to be seen as creative in the fifteenth century, when the Renaissance philosopher Christopher

Landino wrote about the artist as creator, and this concept was slowly adopted. By the seventeenth century, artistic work was labelled "creativity",[50] and the word began to be used for other types of work as well.[51] Human creativity is now seen as an achievement worth celebrating.[52] Marketing agencies, businesses, and schools promote themselves as creative enterprises. We are fascinated by people like Steve Jobs or J. K. Rowling, and want to know the secret of their (very lucrative) talents. Over the last few decades the study of creativity has become a sizeable industry involving a wide range of academic disciplines, all competing to find that magic formula for innovation.

Professor Margaret Boden, a philosopher and psychologist who has spent much of her career investigating creativity, has described two ways to create, which she calls "personal" and "historical". Personal creativity happens when someone does something that is new *for them*. During my life I have learned to play violin pieces, memorized poems, used recipes, and repeated well-known experiments. All of these were moments of personal creativity. None of them were especially original, but they were new to me. Historical creativity, on the other hand, is when somebody does something that *no one* has ever done before.[53] Think Mozart, Monet, and Einstein, or Eminem, Hockney, and Higgs, depending on your tastes.

Creativity, said Boden, is not just about making new combinations of things. "Five hundred and thirty three purple pigs flew over ninety nine orange haystacks" might well be a novel sentence, but it's one that a computer could have created fairly easily using a series of grammatical rules. True personal or historical creativity is about events that are impossible without both conscious effort and the right set of circumstances.

Those circumstances might well include the contribution of other people, not least in science. Newton said that we stand on the shoulders of giants, and that is true for most creative people. Painters adapt established techniques, poets do new things with well-used words, and chefs add a twist of their own to famous dishes. In science, often the timing is right for certain discoveries. Einstein was able to theorize his way to general relativity because others had defined the laws of physics and calculated the speed of light. Mendeleev was able to devise the periodic table because others had already discovered sixty-three chemical elements. Of course individual creativity is important, but science is a collaborative effort with each person building on the work of others.

Another definition of creativity comes from the mathematician and historian of science, Jacob Bronowski. He wrote that both science and art are about discovering hidden likenesses between things, and linking them together.[54] Pablo Picasso and Georges Braque got the idea of drawing using only simple geometric shapes, and invented Cubism. Isaac Newton, home from university during an outbreak of plague, wondered if the planets are affected by the same force as objects on earth, and came up with the concept of gravity. Perhaps technology fits this category too. A person of true genius tried attaching wheels to a suitcase, and one of the greatest problems in human transport was solved.

Nurturing creativity

There must be many more ways to describe creativity, but historically new combinations of things is a good working definition. What we don't understand quite so well is where our creativity comes from. For most people, creativity just happens. Various influences and personality traits come together to produce something that seems to come intuitively. All our words that describe the activity of generating ideas suggest we conjure them from nowhere. "Come up with" is particularly vague.

The word "create" comes from the concept of God creating out of nothing. So human creativity is a paradox, because we are completely incapable of making anything out of nothing. Instead, our thoughts are triggered by what we see around us, memories, or habits we learned when we were young. We tend to use words like intuition or inspiration,[55] as if originality comes from outside ourselves or deep within our subconscious.

I tend to feel more creative in certain environments. I prefer to work by a window overlooking a green space (who wouldn't?), but does what I see outside have a direct effect on my work? Ruth Hogg said that what helps her to be creative is "being willing to read widely, and take an interest in things outside my field, listening to other scientists, and reading scientific biographies – seeing how people got their ideas or made huge leaps".

The novelist Dorothy L. Sayers describes the process of creativity as an outward-moving process.[56] Someone has an experience and then expresses it in some way. She looks at what she has made and recognizes that it communicates her experience. If she fails at the first attempt she might repeat her work until it says what she wants it to say. In order for others to enjoy what has been created, the creator must take a decision to let go and allow it to be interpreted by others.[57] Somebody else then comes along, sees the work, and recognizes an aspect of his or her own life in it. What has been created reminds them of an event they had forgotten, or helps them to recognize an emotion they felt but couldn't express. Sayers' description certainly fits my own experience of the creative process.

Susan Hackwood was a department head in the famously inventive Bell Laboratories, the American telecommunications industry research and development centre in New Jersey. She is now Professor of Electrical Engineering at the University of California, Riverside, and has taken an interest in the cultivation of creativity. She has found that creativity has nothing to do with IQ[58] and you can't inherit it genetically, but it can be nurtured.

Hackwood's formula for creative flourishing includes four ingredients. First there is "autonomous personal vision": the ability to make a project your own and be driven by your own ideals, not those of the people around you. Second is being uninhibited in voicing your new ideas. Third and fourth are the readiness to master new knowledge and skills, and the ability to sustain intense focused effort towards a goal. Hackwood calls these traits and abilities "gifts", as if they are given to certain people, but I think we all have them in some measure, and they can certainly be encouraged to grow.

Time away from gadgets, or "that pokey flashy thing" as

Ruth Hogg's husband calls her tablet, can also help the creative process. A movement is growing in the world of technology, education, and creative thinking to encourage us to switch our gadgets off every now and again. There is evidence that if you let your mind wander while you stand in a queue instead of answering emails on your smartphone, you are more likely to come up with good ideas when you get back to work. The comedian John Cleese describes this approach as making "a tortoise enclosure for your mind". Creativity is a shy animal that takes its time to come out of its shell and get to work, so every now and then we need to make ourselves a calm oasis for uninterrupted thinking.[59]

Ruth told me how she recently spent a frustrating day stranded in an unfamiliar clinic, hoping (in vain) to meet patients who could be part of her latest project. "It just was really difficult. I had no internet access, and the Wi-Fi wasn't working on my phone, so I was stuck in a corner for an entire day trying not to get in anybody's way." The experience wasn't entirely negative, however. "By the end of it I had a whole new idea for writing a grant, and I think that was because I was forced to be alone with my thoughts."

Creativity in community

My final point about creativity, before I move on to theology, is that it happens in community. This is as true for science as it is for any other creative activity. The artist may be alone in his studio, but he might well be about to have lunch with his friends. Steven Johnson, author of *Where Good Ideas Come From*, talks about the slow hunch that needs time to evolve, and which might incubate or lie dormant for many years. Often several ideas need to converge before anything can happen. "Chance favours the connected mind",[60] and networks can play a large part in any creative enterprise.[61]

I loved the film *The Incredibles*, and not just because the idea of discovering my hidden superpowers is quite appealing. My copy of the DVD included a bonus feature about the studio where the film was made, and as I watched I began to recognize some of my own experience in the lab. The staff of Pixar enjoyed and believed in what they were doing, and had all the resources they needed. They had been given the freedom to invent, so they *owned* their work. The result was a set of workspaces decorated with strange memorabilia, teams socializing together, people staying up all night to complete projects, and a fantastic animated movie that pushed the boundaries of what was technologically possible.

My own experience of science, having spent time in five different labs, is similar to what I saw in the Pixar studios. Each place is different, and every team has its own dynamics, but a healthy working environment fosters creative people. Some scientific institutes manage to be exceptionally creative for a time, and the next two examples show how Susan Hackwood's principles for nurturing creativity can be worked out.

Cold Spring Harbor is a hamlet on the North Shore of Long Island about an hour's train ride from New York City. In the 1940s two "enemy aliens" Max Delbrück and Salvador Luria, were excused from war work and given free rein to work there in a lab, which had originally been a biology field station. Delbrück was a German physicist who had developed an interest in biology, and Luria was an Italian medical doctor-turned bacteriologist. They started working on some genetic research using a simple virus called bacteriophage, or "phage", and were soon joined by the bacteriologist Al Hershey. Together they studied the replication mechanism[62] of phage using a synthesis of physics, biochemistry, microbiology, and genetics, and their work laid the foundations for modern molecular biology.

Another significant contribution of this trio, besides their groundbreaking research, was that they invested time in training the next generation of scientists. Delbrück set up a workshop to teach phage techniques to young biologists, and the hugely influential phage course was born. Every summer from 1945 to 1970, college students piled into "small and funky" dorms and labs, working (and partying) their way to scientific greatness. Dress codes were relaxed, but academic rigour was not.

Every student had to pass a difficult maths exam to get onto the phage course, and every presentation they made was ruthlessly critiqued. Many of the same people returned year after year, and the relationships formed through hard work and practical jokes turned into fruitful collaborations. Delbrück, Luria, and Hershey later received the Nobel Prize for their work on bacteriophage, as did twelve former phage course students, and Cold Spring Harbor has remained a centre of excellence for creative science ever since.[63]

Across the Atlantic in Cambridge, the Cavendish laboratory may not have had the party reputation of Cold Spring Harbor (nor the best weather), but it did have a well-established track record for creative science, and boasts twenty-nine Nobel laureates. It was here, in the University of

Cambridge physics department, that phage course graduate James Watson met the brilliant but unconventional Francis Crick, and they worked together on the largely theoretical challenge of understanding the structure of DNA.

Watson and Crick's friendly collaboration involved many hours of conversation, pub lunches, and walks along the river Cam. They closely observed the latest data coming out of various laboratories, and tried out a number of speculative theories. They had molecular models made so they could visualize the different potential solutions, and eventually hit upon something that worked. Others confirmed their prediction with multiple experiments, and Watson and Crick won the Nobel Prize for their efforts. Watson's account of the discovery in his book *The Double Helix* is frank and mildly offensive in places, but it's very readable and a good illustration of the creative, difficult, and at times unexpected process of scientific discovery.

Hopefully these insights have shown more of the human side of science and inspired you to a new level of creativity, whether you are a scientist or not. Creativity can happen both in and outside of the workplace, but the different areas of our lives are interconnected, and for many scientists one of those connections is spiritual. Understanding the importance of creativity in Christian life has helped me to see that a scientist who is also a person of faith can find a good home in the lab.

Faith and creativity

Ruth Hogg has always been interested in exploring the connection between her work and her faith. In Cambridge she was a founding member of the local Veritas Forum, running events to help students and faculty members to discuss – as the Veritas Forum website says – "life's hardest questions and the modern relevance of Jesus Christ". While scientific evidence is important for some, many scientists actually find God outside of the lab: at home, at university, or later in life. Ruth is one of those who discovered God early on, though it was only as an adult that she realized faith and science can fit together.

Growing up in rural Northern Ireland, it was easy for Ruth to accept what she learned about God. "Faith was always part of the way my parents looked at life. Even at school, in my area where the majority of people still went to church, having God as part of your life was very common." With this example, Ruth decided to become a Christian. Later on, at high school and then university, she came across people who didn't believe in God. Ruth heard arguments against Christianity that were a real challenge to her faith, but a positive one. As she worked out answers to these questions and objections, her understanding grew. "Having made a commitment quite young, I did then gradually come to 'own' that decision more myself."

One question remained, however. "I did have a very uneasy feeling about science and Christianity. It was like a Pandora's Box that I was afraid to open, but I knew I had to." This sense of uneasiness remained with Ruth until she spent time as a post-doc in Australia. "That was a time when my faith was probably tested the most, because I realized I was somewhere I could easily leave the whole thing behind if I wanted to. Various personal circumstances had also left me feeling a bit jaded about the goodness of God."

Everything changed when Ruth joined a church in Melbourne. "I had the shock of being in a very evangelical Anglican congregation in Melbourne where I met a lot of people who were really passionate about their faith, and yet science just wasn't an issue for them." Ruth was encouraged to read *The Language of God* by Francis Collins, the former director of the Human Genome Project, who is also a Christian (as mentioned in chapter three).

What Collins said about the relationship between science and faith helped Ruth to make sense of things. "It was so revolutionary to see that I could happily combine my passion for science with a renewed passion for my faith. It was just a huge relief that I didn't have to live in denial." Now, as the leader of a lab, Ruth has more confidence to be open about her faith. She is also able to fully enjoy the "Wow moments, when things fall into place and it's hard not to get a feeling that you're somehow seeing into the mind of God".

I asked Ruth what she thought about creativity in relation to her faith. Although she was very comfortable with the idea of being creative in science, she hadn't thought about it in a Christian context before. There can be an initial fear of creativity in that setting because it might lead to theological mistakes. "You feel that if you're making up new things, then you could get yourself into problems." The reality, as Ruth then said, is that there is a huge amount of creativity happening in the church, especially in music and other art forms.

So how can a scientist like Ruth express their creativity in a faith context? First, there is the creativity of God. "The concept of God as creator is central to Christian faith. It makes sense that we, 'made in his image', have that creative capacity – or more than just a capacity – a real drive to do new things, and find out new things." Ruth also described how her growing understanding of God is, in some ways, a creative process. "In Christian faith you're always learning, through the people you meet and the situations that you come into. You are constantly having to recalibrate your ideas and how you understand your faith, as you see it lived out in other people's lives."

God creates

My theologically trained colleagues tell me that the language of the Hebrew Scriptures is very concrete. It's not surprising, then, that the abstract noun "creativity" never appears directly in the Bible. On the other hand, the creativity of God is a very obvious theme running through the whole text.

The first chapters of Genesis tell how God created in the beginning, making something out of nothing. The scientific story of the universe starts (more or less) with a bang, and then the gradual build-up of more and more complex chemical elements in the bodies of stars. Planets formed, water condensed, and life emerged. Emerged from what? We're not sure. Soup? Ice? Clay? However life began, those first few cells evolved into the countless organisms that now fill the earth. God's immense power sustained and continues to sustain this wonderful development of form and function.

The whole Bible describes God as constantly active in creation: he feeds the lions, makes the wind, and causes the sun to rise. We now know how many of these processes work, but without God's sustaining power nothing would happen, in the same way that turning off the power supply to the TV would result in a blank screen.[64]

The Bible contains images of God creating as an artist or a craftsman, and there's a beautifully poetic example of this in the book of Proverbs. Wisdom is such an important part of God's character that it is sometimes personified. Proverbs 8 describes wisdom as a master worker who was with God as he created the universe.

> I was formed long ages ago, at the very beginning,
>   when the world came to be.
> When there were no watery depths … before the
>   hills, I was given birth …
> I was there when he set the heavens in place,
> when he marked out the horizon on the face of
>   the deep …
> Then I was the master worker at his side.
> I was filled with delight day after day, rejoicing
>   always in his presence,
> rejoicing in his whole world and delighting in the
>   human race.

The first chapter of John's Gospel describes how Jesus was also there at the very beginning, the "Word" through which God created. That makes his decision to come here in human form even more astounding. The creator inhabited his own creation.

The God-man Jesus reflected his Father's character perfectly, so we should expect to see him being creative when he was here. Jesus' adoptive father, Joseph, was a carpenter. In those days a boy learned his father's trade, so Jesus may well have learned to make objects out of wood. His ministry as a travelling teacher began when he was about thirty, so he could have been a very proficient craftsman by then. We don't read in the Bible, "Jesus fixed the table then they all sat down to the Passover meal", or "Jesus visited Simon's mother's house and made her a chair", but if Jesus had carpentry skills, he may have used them – even if the Gospel writers didn't think they were worth reporting.

Jesus was definitely creative in another way, and that was in his teaching. The parables and word-pictures he used to illustrate his points are beautiful and intensely challenging. God's kingdom is like yeast in bread: you can't always see it but it changes everything. The flowers that grow in a field and die in a few days are more magnificently dressed than a king. If God cares for us even more than he cares for the flowers, surely we can trust him to give us what we need? A respected religious leader ignores an injured man on a dangerous road, but a Samaritan[65] – a person Jews would not normally associate with – shows mercy. Every teacher would love to be able to invent such memorable stories.

One of God's ongoing acts of creation is his interaction with people.[66] In the time before Jesus came, God revealed himself through prophets, miracles, and his Law. When people worshipped and prayed to God, he drew near to them. Individuals like David, the Hebrew poet and king, experienced God's presence in their lives. Judging from his writing, it looks as though David might have struggled with depression, but he experienced God's presence in the middle of his illness. In Psalm 40 he wrote, "I waited patiently for the Lord; he turned to me and heard my cry. He lifted me out of the slimy pit, out of the mud and mire; he set my feet on a rock and gave me a firm place to stand. He put a new song in my mouth, a hymn of praise to our God."

A little more than 2,000 years ago, God created something new by sending his Son, who through his teaching, death, and resurrection brought together an eclectic group of people who were the first Christian church. Father, Son, and Spirit choose to work through the worldwide church to create a new way of life: people living life to the full, learning to use freedom wisely, and tackling poverty, disease, and injustice.

So God has revealed himself as a creative being, but what we don't know is exactly how his creativity operates. The most we could do is to extrapolate back from our own experience of creativity, but that is unlikely to be fruitful and might actually be harmful to our theology. Creating God in our image never was a very good idea. I am content to know that God creates, and is therefore creative.

Sub-creators

What about our own creativity? We are evolved creatures, but we are unique. We have a highly developed capacity for imagination, language, and culture. The Bible describes how God brought us into a relationship with himself and gave us responsibility to care for the earth. And as Ruth Hogg has said, although we are unlike God in so many ways, there is a family resemblance: he made us in his own image, and the capacity for relationship and responsibility are an important part of that.[67] Through a long and patient process God has brought us here, and our abilities are a gift to be accepted and cherished, not a power to be wielded and forced.

Ruth's creativity as a scientist and a Christian is inspired by what she sees around her. She said it's hard to compare our creativity to God's because "the extent is just so massively different. You can see so much variety and diversity in the world, and it's hard not to be bowled over by that".

A number of Christian writers have also commented on the differences and similarities between our creativity and the creativity of God. Their insights helped me to see where my own creative contributions – both in science and in other areas – might fit into the grand scheme of things.

Dorothy L. Sayers is famous for her Lord Peter Wimsey detective stories, but she was also an accomplished poet, playwright, essayist, and translator. She wrote on theological themes a number of times, drawing on her own Christian faith. When writing about artistic creativity, Sayers highlighted the fact that only God creates from nothing. "Here there can be no comparison: the human artist is *in* the universe and bound by its conditions. He can create only within that framework and out of that material which the universe supplies."[68]

Sayers also pointed out that creativity must be one of God's most important characteristics, because it is the first thing we learn about him in the Bible. And if we reflect God's image, it's not surprising that we should have some of his creativity. "The characteristic common to God and to man is ... the desire and the ability to make things."[69]

J. R. R. Tolkien, author of *The Hobbit* and *The Lord of the Rings*, was a contemporary of Sayers, and also a Christian. He took the idea of human creativity further, coining the term "sub-creation". We create, he said, because we are somehow like our creator. In *The Silmarillion* he wrote that

> the making of things is in my heart from my
> own making by thee; and the child of little
> understanding that makes a play of the deeds of
> his father may do so without thought of mockery,
> but because he is the son of his father.[70]

Moving to the present century, Adrienne Chaplin is a philosopher of art and a musician who has focused most of her recent work on the relationship between art and Christian faith. Like Sayers, she uses the words "human creativity" cautiously because we cannot create from scratch. Chaplin teaches that we are creatures with God-given gifts, including creativity, and we apply them in different ways to cultivate the world as best we can.[71]

The theologian J. Richard Middleton sums all this up in his book on the image of God. For him, the Genesis account "depicts God as a generous creator, sharing power with a variety of creatures (especially humanity), inviting them (and trusting them – at some risk) to participate in the creative process". In Genesis chapter 2, the sun and moon are to "govern" the day and night, and the earth and waters are invited to "bring forth living creatures". Humans, however, have a special role, "to extend God's royal administration of the world as authorised representatives in earth".[72]

So creativity is clearly an important part of who we are as human beings, and a gift that we should use. What I find most helpful is the humble perspective that all four of these authors give: a reminder that the ultimate source of our creativity comes from outside of ourselves.

The spirit of creativity

The Bible records several episodes of great human creativity. Each of these projects was initiated by God for a specific reason, and involved both scientific knowledge as well as fine craftsmanship.[73] One of the earliest of these was making the tabernacle: a beautiful space in which people could worship God and be aware of his holiness away from other distractions. This work was doubly challenging because the Israelites' nomadic lifestyle at the time meant that anything they built had to be dismantled, packed away, and carried to the next campsite every time they moved. If you have ever been a member of a church that met in a school or other multipurpose public space, you will be familiar with the challenges of mobile worship.

The construction of the tabernacle is described in great detail in the second half of Exodus (chapters 25–30 and 35–40), and it must have been stunning when it was finished. The main tent was made of blue, purple, and red curtains, and surrounded by a large courtyard of fine linen hangings on silver posts. Inside both tent and courtyard was furniture covered in gold, silver, and bronze. Making the tabernacle and all its fittings required great skill and would no doubt have been quite a daunting task, particularly because the instructions God gave left some room for artistic interpretation.

What pattern do you choose for a curtain of linen and

blue, purple, and scarlet yarn? How best to make a gold lamp stand with "cups shaped like almond flowers with buds and blossoms"? What do cherubim look like? God chose Bezalel and "filled him with the Spirit of God, with wisdom, with understanding, with knowledge and with all kinds of skills". He also chose Oholiab as Bezalel's assistant, and gave both of them the ability to teach others. Not content with equipping just two men, God gave "ability to all the skilled workers".[74] These people were skilled in handling different types of materials, which was the advanced science and technology of their day.

Several hundred years after the tabernacle was finished (and no doubt getting decidedly tatty around the edges), the Israelites began a much larger and grander technological project: the construction of a Temple in Jerusalem, led by David's son, King Solomon. This new worship space was built of stone, lined with carved panelling, and covered with gold – including the floor. Like the tabernacle, its furnishings were also covered with precious metals. Solomon's Temple took seven years to build, and was the work of thousands of people. The finished work was both beautiful and functional, a feat of engineering as well as craftsmanship.[75]

Besides these two major projects, God instructed people to carry out a number of creative or symbolic actions throughout the Bible.[76] There is poetry and music, song and dance. Monuments were built, and priests wore beautifully embroidered and jewelled clothes. Perhaps the most original but also the most graphic creative acts were the visual performances by the Old Testament prophets. Jeremiah smashed clay pots, and Isaiah went naked and barefoot for three years. Ezekiel built a model of Jerusalem under siege, lay on his side for a year, and shaved his head. Sometimes God's message to his people was so vitally important and so difficult to swallow that the most extreme and sometimes shocking dramatics were needed to make people pay attention. So there is a very strong biblical mandate for creativity in the arts, crafts, and technology.

Since Jesus came, worship has been transformed. The people of the church are described as being God's Temple, living and working in the world. The great church planter and preacher Paul continued to follow his profession of tent-making alongside his ministry (Acts 18); the writer of the Gospel of Luke is reputed to have been a doctor (Colossians 4); and everyone is encouraged to work with their hands (1 Thessalonians 4:11).[77] Priests and a Temple are no longer necessary, though there is definitely a need for church leaders and beautiful worship spaces.

Redeeming creativity

So far, my writing about creativity has been very optimistic, but not everything we do is good. Every piece of scientific knowledge can be used for constructive or destructive purposes, and it's not always easy to tell the difference. Nuclear fission can be used to generate electricity or make bombs, pesticides save crops but can pollute the environment, and most medicines are harmful in large doses.

Theologians sometimes look at human creativity in one of two ways.[78] The first is to see ourselves as co-creators, not in the specific sense of God limiting himself in order to allow us to create, but because we continue God's act of creation in the world. The second is to focus on the fact that we're not perfect, and what we make is always corrupted in some way. I find the first way of thinking inspiring, but the second is also helpful because it highlights the vulnerability of being human. We need God's help before we can create well.

The Trappist monk and writer Thomas Merton was a good example of someone who put forward a more cautious theology of human creativity. He was concerned about the misuse of artistic talent, and although he was writing in the 1960s, much of his thinking is still relevant today. The first part of his essay, *Theology of Creativity*, describes how an artist can sometimes be elevated to an almost priestly role, though their work might be destructive or self-centred to a point where it can only really be understood by the artist. Merton said that this type of output is not art but self-display. Of course there are thousands of examples of meaningful contemporary art – a number of paintings, books, and documentaries spring to my mind – but the temptation to become selfish is strong.

The second part of Merton's essay is a call to truly creative activity. For him, genuine freedom of expression comes from God, and the only way to stay near to God is to follow Christ. Following inspirational figures has always been important for creative people, and if God is the most creative one (the one who creates from nothing) then there can be no lasting, fully satisfying creativity apart from him. Freedom in obedience may sound like a contradiction, and renouncing our own "limited ends and satisfactions" might seem like a sacrifice, but what is gained is a lasting creativity that "reaches out to the ends of time and to the limits of the universe".

Merton explains his vision of authentic creativity in terms of how we are made. He says that "The image of God in man is his freedom", and that image and freedom is gradually restored through following Christ. This change brings freedom from insecurity, self-centredness, and self-display, and a return to using our God-given gifts for his glory. "The dignity of man is to stand before God on his own feet, alive, conscious, alert to the light that has been placed in him, and perfectly obedient to that light."

This theology of creativity is not just for artists or scientists, because "the creative Christian is not a special kind of Christian, but every Christian has his own creative work to do, his own part in the mystery of the 'new creation'". Neither is creativity about the lone genius. We cannot operate as isolated individuals, because our output affects other people. As Merton says, "situating the person in his right place in relation to other men and to God … would liberate him in the deepest potentialities of his nature…"

Does one need to be a Christian in order to do good creative work in science, fine art, or any other area of life? Of course not, but the temptation to focus on self-display rather than authentic creativity must always be resisted. For scientists like Ruth Hogg, their faith is an important part of what helps them to fulfil their creative potential in the lab.

Conclusion: Living creatively

So being creative is something we all do, though that faculty may be more developed in some than others. I am always happier when I have a creative outlet, whether that involves my work, making music or doing things at home. Nurturing creativity in each other, particularly employees or children in our care, is an important responsibility but one to be borne lightly. We can't *make* ourselves or other people creative – it's a gift that simply needs space to grow.

The creativity of the scientist is in observing closely with as open a mind as possible, then actively pursuing new theories that can be tested in the lab. Devising experiments requires ingenuity and lateral thinking, as well as a good dose of resourcefulness if funding is scarce. Creativity also is an integral part of theology, affecting how we see both God and ourselves. Christians are encouraged to be creative, taking responsibility for their actions, and looking to God to help them steer the course between independent thinking and selfishness.

Creativity is a connection that can help us to have more meaningful discussions about science and faith. How can the creativity of science help us to appreciate the world? What is it about human nature that makes us so creative? How vital is creativity to human flourishing? How much of a responsibility do large organizations – whether scientific or religious – have to foster creativity? How far should we go in encouraging independent thinking? How can theology encourage scientific creativity? How important are different religious faiths in creating truly diverse and creative networks?

I'll give the last word on creativity to Andy Crouch, who happens to be married to a successful scientist.[79] In *Culture Making,* he encourages Christians to recover their creative calling. For some, part of that calling is to do science. Can we be "people who dare to think and do something that has never been thought or done before, something that makes the world more welcoming and thrilling and beautiful"?[80]

Chapter 5

Imagination

... an imaginative or inspirational process enters into all scientific reasoning at every level...

Sir Peter Medawar, biologist[81]

Our visions – our ways of imagining the world – determine the direction of our thoughts.

Mary Midgley, philosopher[82]

Where would we be without our families to embarrass us? I am so used to hearing my parents tell stories about the strange things I did when I was a child that I have taken to sharing these tales myself, and one of them is relevant here. I was an imaginative kid, but around the time of this incident my theory of mind – the ability to imagine oneself into someone else's shoes – was obviously a work in progress. I was playing a game of hide-and-seek with my older brother, and it was my turn to hide. As my brother buried his face and started to count, I vanished.

My ingenious hiding place was in the middle of the room. I simply stood very still – which was a great feat for me at that age – and closed my eyes. I must have been only about two or three years old, but my brother's disgusted, "Ruth, I can still *see* you!" is etched on my memory. I remember exactly where I was standing on the multicoloured seventies leaf pattern carpet in our parents' bedroom. He can still see me. Huh. I ran off to find a better place to hide.

Children inhabit imaginary worlds all the time, but as adults we do so more discreetly. The creative arts are an excellent outlet for grown-up imaginations, but so are many of the tasks we do every day. Gardening, planning holidays, choosing gifts, or cooking meals all involve imagination at some level. Imagination is also an essential part of any intellectual activity.

Creativity is usually an outward act, while imagination happens inside our heads – so the conversation about these two topics is very different, and I felt that each deserved a chapter of its own. While the scientists I spoke to didn't mention imagination directly at first, it is the root of creativity and vital to the practice of science, and I found it impossible to ignore.

My journey into the topic of imagination has also been a particularly personal one. As the possessor of an active imagination, I learned early on that this could be an advantage in some areas, but a disadvantage in others. Problem solving and generating original ideas are essential activities in science, so I enjoyed discovering and developing these abilities during my studies in biology. As a Christian, on the other hand, I had come to see my imagination as a limiting factor – something that got in the way when I should be concentrating on praying or listening to a sermon.

To my great relief, during my research on this topic I discovered a number of scholars who have written about imagination in a Christian context. I hadn't thought about how important imagination is in the prayer, study, and worship that are such a vital part of developing a relationship with God. It turns out that my imagination is just as much of an advantage in faith as it is in science.

I will explore two main ways of thinking about the imagination, using examples from both science and theology. One looks at how imagination can be used to make sense of the world, and the other is about how we keep imagination grounded in reality so that we don't fool ourselves or use it in destructive ways. Here are subjects that are relevant to both scientists and Christians – and those that are both.

While I was writing this chapter I met with Dr Jennifer Siggers, a senior lecturer in the Department of Bioengineering at Imperial College London. I was interested to find out how imagination is relevant to her own subject, and how that works out on a day-to-day basis. I also knew that she was a Christian, having met her at a Christians in Science[83] conference a couple of years before, and I wanted to find out how her experience in science affected (or was affected by) her faith.

After her initial protests that she wasn't sure she had anything to say about imagination, Jennifer spoke with me at some length about how important it is in her work. Her thoughts echoed much of what I had been reading, so I'll include some of her insights as I go through this topic. As I said in my introduction to the last chapter, creativity and imagination are part of the everyday process of science. For a Christian, learning to use imagination in the lab can enhance their faith, helping them to make sense of their experience both in and out of the lab.

Imagining

Attitudes to imagination and how it should be used have varied enormously over the centuries.[84] Different intellectual and cultural movements have come and gone, leaving new ideas and philosophies in their wake. Two of these movements have had a particularly long-lasting impact on society and our view of the imagination, and they are the Enlightenment and Romanticism.[85]

The Enlightenment began in the seventeenth century, led by a number of intellectuals that included David Hume and Adam Smith in Scotland, and Voltaire and Diderot in France. Drawing on the success of the scientific revolution, they wanted to look at the world in a more rational way. Their hope was to solve the problems humankind faced, and create a more harmonious society. For Enlightenment philosophers, both science and religion were activities of the intellect, not imagination.

In the eighteenth century a number of artists, writers, and philosophers began to respond to Enlightenment thinking. They were disillusioned by its overemphasis on rationality and suppressed of emotion, so they started the Romantic Movement. Rationality was still highly valued, but so were creative imagination, individuality, and the expression of emotion. The poets Wordsworth and Coleridge were very influential and so was Turner, whose paintings are still popular today. Many Romantics focused on the beauty of nature, and the feelings of wonder and awe it can bring.

Living in the aftermath of these great cultural movements, we now have a situation where imagination is highly valued in Western culture (the Romantic influence) but not always recognized as an essential part of science (the Enlightenment influence).[86] Perhaps Jennifer's reaction to my invitation for an interview is typical of this: it took her a while to realize how much she had to say about imagination. And as I said in the last chapter, the creative side of science is often hidden from public view – not deliberately, but because it's not usually part of the write-up.

So in drawing attention to the more human side of science, it turns out that this book is something of a Romantic project. The fact that these topics came naturally out of my conversations with scientists shows how thoroughly Romantic values have permeated our society. Of course, my perspective is more biblically based than the Romantic movement generally was. Many Romantics rejected miracles, and saw people as being somehow divine, and many were deists – believing that God doesn't interact with the world. And although I am intrigued by the influence of Romantic philosophy on our thinking, this book is very much about the present, and the way in which scientists today see their Christian faith and their work complementing each other.

Amphibians

Before I move on to the science, I need to define what I mean by "imagination". The act of imagining seems to be instinctive, but what is going on in our minds when we do it? To imagine is to have a mental image, either of something real or invented. You use your imagination to conjure up an idea or a plan for the future. Imagination is what we use for remembering, or to guess what happens next.[87]

Imagination is part of what makes us human. We have the ability look beyond our immediate needs: to dream and invent, tell stories, and search for spiritual realities. Of course, other animals can also be creative in small ways. Many species sing or dance, some build homes, and a few decorate their environment or make tools. Whether these acts are truly creative is open to interpretation, but they seem to be at least a precursor of our own creative activities. There seems to be something distinctively human, however, about our own excessive use of imagination. We interact with other people by imagining how they feel, and choose language we think they will be able to relate to. We can also transcend our physical environment, reflecting on our experiences and finding meaning in life.[88]

Douglas Hedley, a philosopher and theologian at Cambridge University, has thought very deeply about how we use our imaginations. In his book *Living Forms of the Imagination* he describes how, like amphibians, we inhabit two different worlds: the outer, material world, and an inner, mental world of memories and ideals. These worlds are distinct but related, and we have adapted to inhabit both at the same time.

Children are a great example of our amphibious nature. They move seamlessly from real-life situations to imaginary scenarios, and back again. Two little girls might be running down the beach when they come across a log stuck in the sand. Suddenly one of them is a lifeguard heroically rescuing the other from quicksand. They reach the sea and are little girls again, screaming and daring each other to put their feet in the freezing cold water. Then they run back up the sand and one of them becomes a horse and the other is a rider.

As adults we tend to use our imaginations in a less overt way. The imaginary worlds we inhabit are more likely to be memories, problems that need to be solved, or plans for the future. When we make decisions we imaginatively work though different scenarios based on our knowledge of the world and past experience. By transcending our environment we can come up with solutions that seem more promising than others. We are amphibians, Hedley says, moving between the limited world of what our five senses tell us, and "a much vaster domain populated by after-images from memory and projected fears and desires".

Route to reality

Samuel Taylor Coleridge was not only a poet, but he was also a philosopher and critic with great influence in the literary world. Coleridge divided imagination into two categories.[89] The primary or reproductive imagination is to do with seeing things, and ordering them in our memories. I had to use this faculty all the time as a biology student, memorizing diagrams, flow charts, and biochemical reactions.

The secondary or productive imagination transcends the mental order we have created and reorganizes it to make new and deeper meanings. This is where our ideas come from, and is essential for any creative activity. I might study literature, reading Shakespeare, Jane Austen, and Charles Dickens, and remembering their different literary techniques using my reproductive imagination. If I then took that knowledge and let it inspire my own new style of writing, I would be using my productive imagination.

So far, so uncontroversial. Let's push the boat out a bit further. Each of us interprets the world in order to make sense of it. Everything we see or hear is stored away in its chosen cubbyhole. That mental sorting system then feeds back into our thinking. If ice cream is categorized as "food", then when I am hungry I might reach for an ice cream. If, on the other hand, ice cream is pigeonholed as "unhealthy food" I might avoid it. If I associate the sea with "fun" I might go swimming, but if it's sorted under "drowning" I will probably stay well away. In many ways, we imaginatively create the worlds we inhabit.

One important way in which imagination shapes our view of the world is through metaphors, or figures of speech. We collect concepts from everyday life – a journey, an obstacle course, or a prize for good work – and use them to understand situations and express ourselves. Trevor Hart, professor at the Institute for Theology, Imagination and the Arts in St Andrews, has described how these metaphors are then tidied into our mental pigeonholes, but our imagination has fits of untidiness. Life's journey gets mixed up with some of the other metaphors, and we reorganize them to come up with new ways of seeing things.

As Hart put it, we "construct and create an experience that better 'fits' the world".[90] So "life is a journey" could become "life is a journey with many obstacles", or "life is a long journey, but it brings great rewards". Our new imaginative understanding of the world then affects the way we live. I might meet an "obstacle" in life with greater determination, or I would maybe choose to take a risk, because "you never know what's around the corner".

Imagination in science

To find out how these ideas about imagination are relevant to science today, I visited a working scientist. I met Jennifer Siggers on the fourth floor of what was once the Royal School of Mines in South Kensington, just around the corner from the Museums of Science and Natural History. Her office is an inspiring space in a grand corner of London. The windows look out over roofs and domes, and the walls are bare: just a few bookshelves and a whiteboard covered with formulae mark the room out as a place to study.

Jennifer studied maths, specializing in fluid dynamics (the way fluids move) at Cambridge University. During her time as a PhD student she strayed into some seminars on the medical applications of mathematics, and was firmly hooked. She was keen to work on something practical, partly because she liked to have the extra motivation of solving immediate problems to get her out of bed on a bad day. It's also easier to justify medical research than pure maths, so there are more options for funding. Jennifer chose to work on blood circulation through arteries, focusing on the problem of atherosclerosis in heart disease. One of her main research projects now involves studying microcirculation through capillaries in the liver.

When I asked Jennifer about imagination, she said that "science is very creative and you need to have good ideas…

The more you can think out of the box, the better." She gave an example of some modelling she and some of her PhD students had been doing on heartbeat regulation.

Any individual has variations in their pulse rate over the course of a day. These differences might be caused by activity levels, emotions, or simply the action of breathing. There is also a daily cycle of changes in heart rate, with heart attacks being more common just before a person wakes up. A couple of students in Jennifer's group had been comparing heart rate data from healthy individuals and people who have heart disease, to see whether there were any differences in their daily cycles. They thought up some hypothetical scenarios, and then tested those ideas on computer models to see whether they could replicate the differences in heart rate and begin to understand where they might come from.

Most of the previous research had assumed the heart cycles are regular, but the students needed to come up with something better if they were to make any more progress. As Jennifer said, "We always need a bright idea before we can get started." They realized that they could use an analysis method called empirical mode decomposition, which lets the signal choose its own frequency. Their guess proved to be a good one, and they found a 24-hour repeated cycle that looks like a signal from the C.L.O.C.K. gene.[91]

Sometimes what's needed are ideas that are – in Jennifer's words – "a bit wacky", and staring at a blank piece of paper is not always conducive to that sort of thinking. When I asked Jennifer what helped her to be imaginative, she said, "When I was doing my PhD I used to get these sorts of ideas in places like the shower. Now I tend to get them when I'm going to bed or I'm quite relaxed… having thought about the problem deeply and then stopping thinking about it, going home and doing something different, or even on the way home: that can be the time when inspiration strikes."

Jennifer also thinks her environment inspires her ideas. Being next door to so many museums and having an office perched among the rooftops are great perks of her job. She said that "It's impossible to tell whether those things really help or not, but I think they probably do. What definitely helps is walking through the park on my way to work, because I tend to arrive in a good mood… That has been tested!"

Mental science

So having original ideas – or reordering our mental data to make better sense of things – is clearly one of the most important aspects of doing science. The poet Shelley thought a scientist coming up with an idea and a poet writing a verse were doing similar things. He called this process *poiesis*, derived from the Greek word *poiein*, "to create". William Whewell, Master of Trinity College, Cambridge, called these ideas "happy accidents", or "felicitous strokes of inventive talent".[92] Clearly the process of mental reorganization is not a predictable one.

Gerald Holton, a physicist and historian of science from Harvard University, has picked out three other ways in which scientists use imagination, all of which feed into the process of having ideas. The first – and most important – is visual imagination, which scientists use to create mental pictures or models. Just before I met Jennifer she had been using mental pictures to help solve an equation. She was breaking it down, using a different physical concept to visualize the effect of each mathematical term. So diffusion is when things spread out, decay means things drop off, and so on. After adding a new term, she would check the equation to see if it had the effect she had envisaged. It turns out that even mathematics isn't completely abstract in practice.

A model is a more elaborate kind of mental picture that makes sense of a whole collection of data. When James Watson and Francis Crick were working on the problem of DNA structure, they had an idea that it was a double-stranded molecule. They looked at data from DNA crystallization experiments and started coming up with ideas about its structure. They tested each of their ideas mathematically, and talked over the different structural models that might work. Eventually they made their mental models real, building them to scale out of pieces of metal and lab equipment. A model was found that seemed to fit the data, so they published it. Others confirmed their prediction with experiments, and – as I mentioned in chapter four – Watson and Crick then won the Nobel Prize.

Sometimes models can be tested imaginatively using thought experiments – stories about imaginary worlds where different theoretical scenarios are played out. Schrödinger's cat is locked in a box. Inside the box is a vial of poison hooked up to some radioactive material. When the radioactive substance decays – even just a single atom – the poison will be released and the cat will die. (No one said thought experiments had to be nice.) So there are two possible logical outcomes: the cat will either live or die.

Schrödinger devised his imaginary box experiment to demonstrate how some aspects of physics can be counterintuitive. According to the physicists who proposed "superposition", the cat is in both states simultaneously until you look inside. When you lift the lid reality collapses into one possibility or the other, and you discover a cat that is either dead and radioactive, or alive and pleased to see daylight.

In the end, thought experiments should be tested with lab experiments, and thankfully the elaborate cat apparatus was not necessary to test whether the idea of superposition is correct. In specialist electrical circuits, some subatomic particles can exist temporarily in two states: a result that has proved useful in communications and computer technology. So the imaginary cat-in-a-box was an important stage in scientific enquiry, and theoretical physicists continue to use this type of mental gymnastics as part of their work.[93]

The second way scientists use their imaginations is in creating parallels or analogies. Some scientific concepts are difficult to describe with words so we use everyday examples to illustrate them. The analogy of a swing is helpful for Jennifer Siggers when she's thinking about heart rhythms. The swing has its regular rhythm but it gets out of synch and has to be reset (by pushing the swing) every day. Another analogy for Jennifer comes from the human body. "A lot of researchers will think of our blood circulation system as being like a big electrical circuit with a battery, which is the heart sending off signals. So resistance (slowing down of the current) represents how long and narrow the arteries are, and capacitance (ability to store charge) represents their elasticity."

The third and final way of imagining in science, according to Holton, is the assumptions we bring to it: our mental pigeonholes. Einstein thought his equations should show symmetry, unity, and continuity, and although these ideals led him to make some mistakes later in his career, he didn't regret having them to start with. He said trying to work without assumptions would be like trying to breathe in a vacuum. We need an imaginary framework within which to start making sense of the world, even if that framework is replaced by something else later on by a bold leap of imagination.[94]

Jennifer said that in every project, she starts off with a list of assumptions and chooses a model to work with, but further down the road she might realize it's not working. "It could be that we spent a long time getting to that point, and then realize one of our assumptions doesn't work..." Having to give up a cherished idea can, Jennifer admitted, "quite often be a bit heartbreaking", but it "happens absolutely all the time. That's part of the process."

Testing

So the route to reality in science is through forming and reforming our mental pictures of the world, testing them each time with experiments. The biologist Sir Peter Medawar described a hypothesis (an idea about the way things might work) as "an imaginative preconception of what the truth might be". The scientist's job, says Medawar, is then to do experiments that are "designed to find out whether this imagined world of our hypothesis corresponds to the real one".[95]

This approach of hypothesizing and testing is one we often use in other areas of life, although experiments are replaced with life experience or other kinds of knowledge. What sorts of birthday presents does my brother enjoy? What does a healthy relationship look like? How much stress can I handle before I need a break? As amphibians, we need to constantly move between our inner and outer worlds, testing which of our ideas are good and which need to be revised or jettisoned completely.

C. S. Lewis described this process of sifting ideas in his imaginatively titled essay, "Bluspels and Flalansferes". He said that "imagination is the organ of meaning", because it is the source of all metaphors. Is my love a red, red rose or a bloodsucking vampire? Is DNA like a blueprint or a set of switches? Once a number of potential meanings are on the table, then reason – "the natural organ of truth" – looks at the information available from both our inner and outer worlds, and judges between them. So imagination is not the enemy of reason, as some Enlightenment philosophers thought, but the two work together. Reason needs imagination before it can get started, and imagination needs reason to keep it in check.

Those who are tempted to overlook imagination in science must be careful. In mathematics, zero and negative numbers were largely ignored in Europe until at least the eighteenth century. Most people thought they were meaningless, despite the fact that Indian mathematicians had been using them for over 1,000 years. Even more difficult to grasp were "imaginary numbers", which are now standard practice in several areas of science, including electromagnetism and fluid dynamics.[96]

One of the first people to use imaginary numbers was the

sixteenth-century mathematician Rafael Bombelli. When he wrote about them he knew his readers would be sceptical, so he was brutally honest. He explained that he too had thought using imaginary numbers was just a way of trying of look clever, but he tried hard to understand them and found that they were mathematically correct. So he warned his audience, saying that "let the reader apply all his strength of mind, for [otherwise] even he will find himself deceived".[97] In other words, failing to engage your whole mind on a problem, including your imagination, is a way of closing your eyes to reality.

God and imagination

For scientists like Jennifer Siggers, this process of hypothesizing and testing – both in and out of the lab – leads them to God. Jennifer said that "science makes much more sense if there is, at some deep level, a truth that we're pursuing". For her, mathematics has its origin in God. Through her work she is "discovering what he's already put there, and it's absolutely beautiful". When she uses her imagination to tackle a problem in bioengineering, she expects to discover something. "The fact that I believe in a God makes me confident that there's an answer to any scientific question we're asking. Whether we'll find it, I don't know, but there *is* an answer."

Some people think that, like creativity, having an imagination is part of what it means to be "made in the image of God". God's creativity is an underlying theme of the Bible, but is imagination? God created the universe, which could have been an imaginative act, but while we have to use our imaginations to guess the future outcome of our own creations, doesn't God just *know*?

We create new things using materials, concepts, and ideas gleaned from the world around us and our experience of it. We explore the universe and try to understand it. We attempt to understand other people and their needs, and we try to grasp the reality and character of God. All of these activities stretch our imagination to the utmost but what if, in doing these things, we are using a faculty that God doesn't actually need much of the time?

I believe that God knows the universe, knows us, and knows himself completely. We "see only a reflection as in a mirror" (1 Corinthians 13:12) because we have finite minds, and are bound by time and space. In the end, we shall see God "face to face", and though we may still be limited, perhaps we will have less need for imagination. What if our active imaginations – that are so involved in striving to understand events and plan for the future – are not so much a reflection of God's character, but a gift to help us get on with our lives?

Imagination in Christianity

So imagination is not just important in theology, but in all of Christian living. I have found three main ways in which Christians use their imaginations, and they happen to be similar to the ways in which imagination is used in science.

First, there are several kinds of mental images. Perhaps the best example of this is scriptural meditation, which involves visualizing a scene from the Bible or imagining yourself to be one of the people there. The writer and theologian Richard

Foster described this technique in his much-loved book *Celebration of Discipline*. We are encouraged to

> apply all our senses to the task. Smell the sea.
> Hear the lap of water along the shore. See the
> crowd. Feel the sun on your head and the hunger
> in your stomach. Taste the salt air. Touch the hem
> of [Jesus'] garment.

We are not passive observers, but active participants in the story.

I have found that inhabiting the story for myself is a way to become aware of the full implications of Jesus' teaching for my own life. Like scientific imaginings, I can't learn anything new from this sort of exercise, but I can understand it more deeply. As William Loader says in *The New Testament with Imagination*, "There are no wild flights of imagination, no making up of stories, just reflections of what we already know, but seen from a likely perspective within the scene." This is the most important form of Christian meditation and requires time, imagination, and humility – facing God is not easy.

Thought experiments are also used in a Christian context. Pastors and theologians often take the truths of the Bible (our data) and use them to create imaginary scenarios that help us understand God more deeply. I recently heard a sermon where the speaker asked us to imagine that Jesus was going to be physically present in our church for one day, and all the joy and uproar that would cause. Having imagined that scene, we were told that the Holy Spirit is equivalent to Jesus' presence with us – though of course without a physical body. The striking mental image of Jesus in our church building was enough to drive home the point.

Psalm 139 includes a thought experiment about the mind of God: "How precious to me are your thoughts, God! How vast is the sum of them! Were I to count them, they would outnumber the grains of sand – when I awake, I am still with you." The picture the psalmist paints of his own slumbering on the job creates a beautiful image. It's almost as if the counting continues throughout the night as he sleeps, and when it's over he awakes to enjoy God's presence.

Second, analogy and symbol are also important in Christianity. God is spirit, so we need concrete ways to remind ourselves about him. Two examples straight from the pages of the Bible are the bread and wine in communion that symbolize Jesus' body and blood in his death and resurrection. Then there is the baptism of each new Christian, symbolizing death to an old way of life and rebirth to a new. Every group of worshipping Christians has also created its own particular symbols: incense and coloured vestments in high churches, jeans in low churches,[98] and a huge diversity of crosses. Just as a wedding ring signifies a real relationship, so these symbols of the church communicate deep truths in terms we can both grasp and remember.

Another very powerful set of analogies are found in Jesus' teaching.[99] Discovering God is like finding a priceless pearl. We should be like the "good Samaritan". God loves us like the best kind of father. Jesus used these stories to capture the imagination of his audience, and drive home his point in a very memorable way. A man sold all he had to buy that pearl. The devout Jewish leader ignored a man's cries for help, but the Samaritan (and an enemy of the Jews) had compassion. The profligate and disgraced son turned back to his father and was welcomed home with a party. It's no wonder that so many of these stories and ideas have made their way into popular culture.

Christians down the centuries have continued Jesus' tradition, using stories to illustrate their points. Perhaps the most important use of analogy in Christian theology is in descriptions of atonement.[100] This is the belief that because we are unable to make amends for the wrong we do, God took matters into his own hands. A popular illustration of this is a judge in a court of law. He hands over a fair sentence, and then walks into the dock to pay the penalty himself. In other stories, the cross is a bridge between us and God, or the shepherd lays down his life for the sheep (Jesus used that one).

Some scientists are opposed to using visual illustrations in science,[101] but it's impossible to avoid using them because that's the way we understand the world. The same applies to a Christian's understanding of God. I can only think about him through metaphors, but I need to remember that God is more real than even the best imaginative illustration of his character. Human fatherhood is a picture or shadow of God's fatherhood, and not the other way around.

When it comes to imagination, science can enhance faith. Jennifer Siggers explained how this works for her. "I definitely bring a lot of the skills from my work into things that I do with church. For example, when I explain Bible passages to people, something I almost always do is to make an analogy to try and bring the passage alive to the listeners in a new way. As I do this it helps me to understand the meaning better, because I've created an illustration and in doing so had to think about whether it conveys the right meaning. When I do this, I often have to drop a few of them, because I've thought, actually that's not really what it's like. The story isn't quite trying to convey that theme. That is very similar to aspects of the process of research."

Sense-making

The last use of imagination in Christianity is in making sense of what we experience. According to the theologian and scientist Alister McGrath, there are signs in nature that point beyond themselves to another reality: to God. The order we see in the universe, the fact that we can understand it, the emergence of life, and our own experience of spirituality are not proof for God, but for many people they point to his existence. When you look at how things are in nature, the God hypothesis makes the most sense.

Douglas Hedley writes that "In the Scriptures, faith tends to be opposed to sight, not to knowledge".[102] If "sight" is similar to science – the desire to see hard evidence for something – then what God does can go beyond scientific knowledge. There are limits to the type of questions science can answer, but there are other types of knowledge – particularly where relationships are concerned. As Hedley says, "Just as we use the imagination to relate to other minds, appreciate beauty and understand goodness, we need imagination to engage with God's action in the world."[103] It's impossible to understand a person without imagining yourself into their shoes, and a similar exercise is needed to engage with God. Imagination, "for all its pitfalls and limitations, can be the vehicle of 'awakening' to an invisible world".[104]

Some people would label this type of imagining as "fancy" (dreaming up imaginary worlds), but Hedley disagrees. He thinks that human curiosity reflects something real about the world. "We seek order, and we find it."[105] One scientific technique that I mentioned in chapter two was inference to the best explanation. Any data set can be interpreted in a number of ways, and the challenge then is to decide which interpretation is the most correct. This sorting of possibilities and running of mental scenarios requires imaginative judgments and intuition, and Christian thinking requires the same skills.

Freedom of imagination

So both imagination and creativity are part of the process of doing science, theology, and life in general. I have already written about true freedom in creativity, but what about imagination? Scientists are cautious about imagination, and so are theologians,[106] which is good because both types of people influence the way many people live their lives. Whether I am trusting the scientific principles behind technology or deciding how to live our lives, I want to avoid being misled. We can also mislead ourselves. I can use my imagination to make sense of the world in a productive way, but the undirected imagination can lead to some very dark places.

Douglas Hedley calls the wrong use of imagination "fantasy": not the type of fantasy we use to entertain children or explore truths about life, but a way of fooling ourselves that can lead to destructive behaviour. He writes that "Selfishness, anxiety, cruelty, fanaticism and superstition are products of fantasy … Fantasy creates a substitute domain for the empirical world … and is frequently marked by a poverty of imaginative possibilities." In other words, a failure to balance active imagination with reason, sifting ideas and testing them against our experience of the world, has consequences both for ourselves and for the rest of the world.

Rowan Williams, the former Archbishop of Canterbury, summed all this up when he wrote that sin is simply "the condition of being seriously wrong about reality". He went on to say that our perception of reality is naturally skewed, so we need to keep asking ourselves awkward questions. Is that the best interpretation of the data? Is my new idea useful? Am I understanding that person properly? Developing this constant awareness is not easy. We can't just rely on our own resources, but we also can't always rely on our surroundings to help us.

Every individual has had their imagination trained in different ways – either positive or negative – by family, education, and culture. That process is ongoing, and at times irresistible. The humble recognition that we can't pull ourselves up by our own bootlaces, said Williams, is the beginning of the way back to reality and true freedom of imagination. One illustration of this comes from C. S. Lewis's own experience.

As a young man, Lewis believed that the world was a "meaningless dance of atoms".[107] Finding this view of life somewhat depressing, he bought a novel on a train station, hoping to cheer himself up. The book he found was

Phantastes by the Scottish writer George MacDonald, which is a story about a young man who explores another world, has a number of adventures, and learns about himself through them. For Lewis, this book was a wake-up call that enabled him to see the good at the heart of things, and drew him out of his loneliness to connect with the world around him. He later wrote that this book "baptised" his imagination. "Rather than leading him into an escape *from* reality, it washed away blinding scales and gave him a new vision *of* reality."[108] He said that it showed him "the quality of the real universe, the divine, magical, terrifying and ecstatic reality in which we all live".[109]

The best kind of fiction challenges and inspires without indulging in either blind materialism or romantic escapism. It can help us to regain a balanced view of the world as a place of suffering, but filled with hope. Perhaps this is what Rowan Williams meant when he wrote that "We need the tightening circle of our unreality to be interrupted ... whether through someone's life, or a work of art, or just ... the experience of solitude".

The question remains, how did MacDonald train his own imagination? MacDonald was a minister, and for him, the wise imagination was the "presence of the Spirit of God".[110] He believed that "To enquire into what God has made is the main function of the imagination",[111] but the imagination needs to be fed. As the writer of Philippians (4:8) said, "whatever is true, whatever is noble, whatever is right, whatever is pure, whatever is lovely, whatever is admirable – if anything is excellent or praiseworthy – think about such things."

Our creativity reflects God's creative power in some way, and imagination plays a vital role. God's good creation included us in it, flourishing as people and enhancing what he has made by sharing in his creativity. What C. S. Lewis glimpsed in MacDonald's book was the reality of a restored connection with God, and the freedom of imagination that came from being brought back into contact with reality. As the theologian and philosopher Francis Schaeffer said, "The Christian is the really free man ... the one whose imagination should fly beyond the stars."[112]

Science and theology

Freedom of imagination is as important in science as it is in Christianity. I have found two examples that show how the interaction between theology and imagination can affect progress in science, and they are both to do with honest observation and building up a picture of the world that makes the best sense of the data. This is a demonstration of how science can enhance faith, and faith can enhance science.

Our brains have to make assumptions, because if we noticed everything all the time we wouldn't have the processing power to handle it all. Moment to moment, what we see of a scene is our memory of it, plus or minus anything that has changed. Some things we "see" might be enhanced or removed by our imagination, depending on our fears and expectations. So a tree becomes a bear, a flier under my windscreen wiper becomes a parking ticket, and I don't notice that my bag is on the roof of the car.[113]

So to be successful, a scientist must look more closely and be more observant than most. The astronomer Galileo was good at this. He observed the moon with his telescope, and saw a lot of lumps and bumps at the edge of the earth's shadow on the surface of the moon. We now know that these irregularities are caused by craters and mountains, but Galileo was the first to actually notice them.

Other astronomers before Galileo had not seen the mountains on the moon, perhaps because telescopes at that time were so primitive that they didn't trust what they saw. The other reason, according to Gerald Holton, was because they were influenced by Greek philosophy. Aristotle had taught that the moon is perfectly spherical, symbolizing the incorruptible universe. And in the Middle Ages, the image of a perfectly spherical moon was used to symbolize the immaculate conception of the virgin Mary. So the astronomers' imaginations, influenced by these philosophical or religious ideas, had got the better of them. Galileo was different. He trusted his eyes and reported what he saw. Before long, others began to notice the same things, and the spherical, symbolic moon was forgotten.

Galileo's drawings of the moon

Professor Andrew Wyllie, the former head of the Department of Pathology at Cambridge University, is another example of seeing effectively, and not being distracted by imaginative assumptions. This time, his Christian faith helped him to see more clearly.

As a PhD student, Wyllie used electron microscopes to study different types of tissues. He was interested in the regulation of cell numbers during growth, and how cell death might play a part in that. He noticed that during normal development, some cells undergo a very tightly controlled sequence of dying and being swallowed up by phagocytes (the type of white blood cells that clean up unwanted particles from the body). This process of programmed cell death was named apoptosis,[114] and we now know that it is crucially important in the development of an embryo. If apoptosis hadn't happened during your early life, your fingers and toes would be webbed, not to mention the effects on your heart, brain, and spinal cord.

I spent several months of my Masters degree working on apoptosis, so I was excited to hear Wyllie speak at The Faraday Institute for Science and Religion.[115] After describing his part in the discovery of apoptosis, he explained how his faith had helped him to recognize and accept the evidence for this process. Wyllie thinks that his eyes were open to apoptosis because he wasn't afraid of death – for a Christian, it's not the end of the story. The fact that death might be part of life for us just now wasn't something that fazed him, so he spent time recording and studying what he saw. It took others in the scientific community much longer to accept the idea, but it was eventually recognized as an important contribution to science.

Conclusion: Fulfilled amphibians

So we use our imaginations to build up a picture of the world, and hopefully a realistic one. We pigeonhole things, then rearrange them to make better sense of what we know, or create new ideas. We move amphibiously between our inner and outer worlds, testing our ideas against our experience of the world and other people.

Thinking about imagination in this way can be a bit mind-bending, but I have found it a helpful way of making sense of both science and faith. I am now more aware of the ways in which imaginative thinking can help or hinder the way I live my life. I have also been inspired by Jennifer's work, and the way it complements her faith.

Of all the chapters in this book, this one has been the most challenging to write – but it might also be the most important. It breaks down the traditional barriers between science and faith, showing that they have something in common. Both enterprises use imagination, and that is part of the joy of study. Exercising creativity, coming up with ideas and trying them out is one of the greatest rewards of these disciplines. They both have checks and balances to keep our thinking realistic, although the aspect of reality that each subject focuses on is completely different.

The Cambridge paleobiologist[116] Simon Conway Morris is my final example of a scientist who uses his imagination to the full. Remembering and classifying countless fossilized organisms from different locations around the world is a great exercise in visual imagination. Coming up with ideas about how those animals and plants might be related to each other, and to living things today, is even more challenging.

Conway Morris has challenged the prevailing idea that evolution is directionless, and proposed that it might actually be a more predictable process than some people think. In similar environments, the same highly optimized structures evolve time after time. For example, detecting light is useful, and lenses are a good way to channel light into the body, so "camera eyes" like ours have evolved independently about seven times. The path of evolution has converged on the same solution, over and over again.

It can be difficult to find the balance between coming up with original (or wacky, to use Jennifer Siggers' word) ideas and testing them against reality, but it is worth the risk. In his introduction to the book *The Deep Structure of Biology*, Conway Morris wrote:

> … as all scientists know, the path between
> inspiration and self-delusion can be painfully
> narrow. Yet I must emphasise that biology like
> any science can only progress if the ideas are
> adventurous, and nobody can complain if a
> hypothesis fails to survive the rigours of peer
> review[117] – or alternatively leads to a Nobel.

Many other scientists are now working in the area of evolutionary convergence, their ideas are being sifted thoroughly, and we can look forward to finding out some interesting things in the years to come.

Conway Morris is also a Christian, and is fully aware that his work has theological implications. This is where the barriers between science and theology really start to come down: not just because both use imagination in similar ways, but because they can also lead to similar questions. Conway Morris is cautious about making statements about evidence for God, but in the *Test of FAITH* documentary he invited the audience to think about whether the "claims made by particular religious traditions" might be "in any way congruent with" the picture of the world that comes from this area of science.[118]

Theologians test their ideas against what we know of God's character and plans from the Bible, and our interactions with God throughout history. They must also pay attention to the world we live in, how it works, and what happens to us. Are new theological ideas consistent with these realities? So far, Christian theology seems to make sense of convergent evolution. It makes sense of the fact that intelligent beings have emerged that can understand and analyse the universe; that they have come up with a number of alternative ways of seeing the world; that they grasp those worldviews imaginatively and allow them to shape the way they see themselves and their surroundings; that they can relate to each other and make music and art, or study science and theology. Perhaps other hypotheses will be proposed, and they will be tested against that same reality.

Having looked at the process of doing science, the next three chapters are about the outcome: the beauty, wonder, and awe that a scientist might feel when they discover new things. All of these experiences involve imagination in different ways, and the connection with theology remains. Scientific discovery raises questions that go beyond science.

So I will finish with a word from Blaise Pascal, a French scientist whose talents included physics and mathematics. He invented the calculator, collaborated with the famous mathematician Fermat (of Fermat's last theorem), and in his thirties he decided to devote the rest of his life to philosophy and theology. In his book, *Pensées* (thoughts), he described an imaginary journey through the immensity of the universe, immersing himself in the vast scales of astronomy. For Pascal, scientific knowledge enhanced his faith by expanding his mental picture of the world:

> Let man then contemplate the whole of nature
> in her full and lofty majesty, let him turn his gaze
> away from the lowly objects around him; let him
> behold the dazzling light set like an eternal lamp
> to light up the universe, let him see the earth as a
> mere speck compared to the vast orbit described
> by this star, and let him marvel at finding this vast
> orbit itself to be no more than the tiniest point
> compared to that described by the stars revolving
> in the firmament. But if our eyes stop there, let
> our imagination proceed further; it will grow
> weary of conceiving things before nature tires of
> producing them. The whole visible world is only
> an imperceptible dot in nature's ample bosom.
> No idea comes near it; it is no good inflating our

conceptions beyond imaginable space, we only bring forth atoms compared to the reality of things. Nature is an infinite sphere whose centre is everywhere and circumference nowhere. In short it is the greatest perceptible mark of God's omnipotence that our imagination should lose itself in that thought.[119]

Chapter 6

Beauty

*I belong in the ranks of those who have cultivated
the beauty that is the distinctive feature of scientific
research.*

Marie Curie, physicist and chemist[120]

*If the heavens really are "telling the glory of God",
this implies that something of God can be known
through them…*

Alister McGrath, theologian & biophysicist[121]

As a biologist I am fascinated by the images of cells, protein
structures, and weird and wonderful organisms that grace the
covers of scientific journals. I have spent whole weeks staring
down a microscope at the beautifully transparent bodies of
developing fish embryos, and whenever possible I illustrate
my written work with photographs of the natural world.

I'm not alone in my love of the visual side of biology.
In the institute where I did my PhD we had a basement
full of microscopes and digital imaging technology, and
we impressed each other with beautiful pictures in our
presentations – movies were even better. The journal *Nature
Cell Biology* always features striking images, and in an editorial
these photographs were described as works of art in their own

right.[122] Displays of science-related pictures or sculptures are increasingly popular in research institutes, museums, science festivals, and other public spaces. I even have a book on my desk called *Hidden Beauty in Medicine* that is full of (oddly) beautiful pictures of diseased tissue.

If creativity and imagination are essential to the practice of science, then beauty, wonder, and awe are some of the driving forces that help scientists to stay motivated. The appearance of beauty down the microscope or on the computer screen can help them to enjoy the mundane side of their work – and when the final results come in, the overall picture may be beautiful too. In this chapter I will explore what it is that scientists find beautiful, what questions beauty may provoke, and what beauty might tell us about God.

Science-art

As well as tracking down a working scientist who is a Christian to contribute to this chapter, I also spoke to an artist. Dr Lizzie Burns[123] trained as a cell biologist and worked in a cancer research lab for several years at Oxford University, but she has always loved drawing, painting, and making things. When Lizzie exhibited some of her paintings in the biochemistry department, the feedback she received was so positive that she began to think about a career in scientific art. She now earns a living running workshops and producing paintings, photographs, and even jewellery with scientific themes.

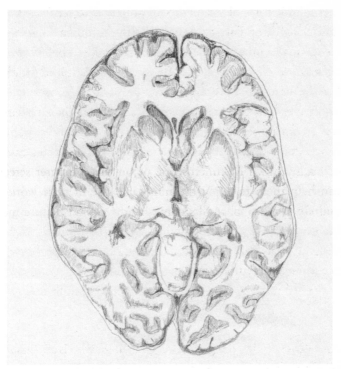

Inner Workings © Dr Lizzie Burns

Now that she has a foot in both art and science, Lizzie has realized that artists and scientists have different attitudes to beauty. While beauty is a tool that artists may or may not choose to use to explore, scientists can simply be fascinated by beauty in nature and celebrate it in any way they can.

Lizzie is fascinated by the hidden and very complex view of life at the cellular and molecular levels. Through her art she is able to show how incredible life is, and why scientists are so fascinated by the subjects they study. It is difficult to grasp how wonderful the processes of our bodies can be, even when they go wrong, so beautiful pictures can help to communicate this. Something that could potentially be quite disgusting, or an unwelcome reminder of our mortality, is completely amazing when you look at it under the microscope. Art can also be used to explore the very personal side of science, preserving something as intimate as a twelve-week baby scan.

In recent years, explaining science to the general public has become an essential part of a scientist's role. Most researchers are required by their departments to spend time outside of the lab, working with people like Lizzie to explain the relevance, as well as the beauty and wonder of science, to the general public. I was involved in the Edinburgh Science Festival as a PhD student, creating exhibits and running experiments for children. I loved this side of my work, and I have tried to bring some of that experience to this book.

Beautiful worms

In preparation for writing this chapter, I sat in on another lab meeting, this time in the US. I met Professor Jeff Hardin at the University of Wisconsin-Madison, where he is chair of the zoology department and teaches cell and developmental biology. He and the members of his lab study a tiny (1 millimetre long) transparent roundworm called *Caenorhabditis elegans* (*C. elegans*), which shares many of the most basic functions of our own bodies.

The average human body contains around 50 trillion cells.[124] *C. elegans*, on the other hand, has about 1,000. When a human embryo grows, its cells divide rapidly and take on different properties, forming all the tissues needed for its body. This process – called differentiation – is tightly controlled, but it would be impossible to predict the fate of every individual cell in a developing human. In little *C. elegans*, however, it has been possible to map out the fate of all 959 of its cells,[125] including 131 that died along the way.

So the life of this small organism is completely prescribed: hatch, grow, moult four times, then mate. Most *C. elegans* adults are hermaphrodites, so they make some sperm, then switch to making eggs and fertilize themselves. One could find this cycle depressing, but that's not the take-home message for Hardin. "Knowing the steps in a complicated bit of ballroom dancing leads to greater appreciation for the skill of the dancers, and it is the same with *C. elegans*. Watching these tiny embryos in exquisite detail using powerful microscopes gives us a deep sense for the intricate cellular choreography that builds their bodies."

In his lectures on developmental biology Jeff quotes Psalm 139, a piece of ancient Hebrew poetry. The writer – thought to be King David of Israel – is musing about embryonic development, and using poetic language to talk about how his body was formed. Hardin said that he appreciates this psalm because "David doesn't understand the process of how his body was formed, but he knows that it's wonderful."

Hardin tells his students, "Whether you share David's worldview – as I as a Christian happen to – or not, by the end of the semester I want you to share his sense of wonder about the incredible intricacy of developmental biology and the processes that we have the privilege of studying." In the teaching evaluations at the end of the semester there are usually comments from the students about this, saying, "Wow, he actually cares about this material." I found Hardin's enthusiasm for his work infectious and inspiring, and I will return to his thoughts at various points throughout the chapter.

What is beauty?

After my conversations with Jeff and many others, I can safely say that it appears to be a universal experience for a scientist to find beauty in the objects he or she studies. A cynical person might say that this is because the daily discipline of examining *anything* in detail helps us to appreciate its finer points. Or maybe the process of choosing something to work on and then spending the greater part of your waking hours staring at it provokes something akin to the loyalty of a mother who thinks her child is beautiful, despite the large pimple on its nose.

The scientist's experience of beauty seems to be more than just the fascination and devotion of the true professional, but before I can make my case I need to define "beauty". Definitions in different times and cultures have been varied and contradictory, including symmetry, harmony, proportion, order, unity, a ratio of uniformity to variety, uselessness, and usefulness. Plato and some of his contemporaries considered beauty to be a virtue, part of a trio with goodness and truth.[126]

The German philosopher Alexander Gottlieb Baumgarten coined the term "aesthetics" in the 1750s to describe an extremely old field of study: the analysis of how we understand the world through our senses (sight, hearing, etc.). This term was adopted by other thinkers, who used it to refer to beauty in particular. Eventually aesthetics became its own field of study, and defining beauty became even more difficult.[127]

Is beauty in the eye of the beholder, or a fixed quality? Is beauty a rare quality – something that takes your breath away – or can it be found in an everyday object that is quite plain but simple and satisfying?

When it comes to natural beauty, the biologist E. O. Wilson and a number of others have connected our ideas of beauty with evolutionary history. We enjoy wide-open vistas, long stretches of clear water, hiding places, and high lookout points because they would help us to survive in a wilderness situation.[128] Other aspects of aesthetics are no doubt related to our culture, upbringing, or personal preference. I also wonder whether we enjoy nature and find it refreshing because it is so much more complex than anything we can make ourselves.

My own definition of beauty for the purposes of this chapter is "something that is pleasing to the senses". This can include more abstract qualities that appeal to the intellect as well as the emotions. So a tree might be beautiful because it's covered in blossom, but also because it has an unusually symmetrical shape. A new bike might be beautiful because it's red and shiny and desirable, but also because it is well designed. I assume that beauty is a matter of taste most of the time, but will mention a few people who think it is an indicator of truth.

Seeing

Whatever the reasons might be for our appreciation of beauty, the essential first step is to notice it. Training our senses to a higher degree of observation can bring great rewards, and this is something that poets practise as well as scientists. As a student I spent many lab sessions staring down microscopes and drawing what I saw. Despite my best efforts the end result was often a greyish mess, but it taught me how to look at things properly and notice the details.

W. H. Davies' poem "Leisure" encourages the cultivation of a deliberate habit of unhurried observation:

> What is this life if, full of care,
> We have no time to stand and stare.
>
> No time to stand beneath the boughs
> And stare as long as sheep or cows ...
>
> No time to see, in broad daylight,
> Streams full of stars, like skies at night ...

Another favourite of mine is Elizabeth Barrett Browning's slightly caustic observation in her book-length poem *Aurora Leigh*. "Earth's crammed with heaven, And every common bush afire with God; But only he who sees, takes off his shoes, The rest sit round it and pluck blackberries..."

I wasn't surprised to find out that Jeff uses the *Aurora Leigh* quote in his classes. He said, "My students don't understand how incredible developmental biology is, so my goal in teaching is that they would not be of the sort that are sitting around picking blackberries."

So when he teaches his students, Jeff starts by telling them that his main goal for the semester is that they would think cells and embryos are amazing. He uses a quote from Albert Einstein: "He [or she] to whom this emotion is a stranger, who can no longer pause to wonder and stand rapt in awe, is as good as dead…"[129] Jeff wants his students to be much better than dead by the end of the semester!

Jeff is also a fan of the nineteenth-century nature writer Henry David Thoreau, another man who believed in observing nature deeply. In response to a collection of his essays Hardin wrote:

> What can a practicing scientist in the 21st century
> – even a "bench scientist" like me whose scientific
> forays are confined to a laboratory – glean
> from a 19th century wanderer like Thoreau? …
> attentiveness to nature involves a particular way of
> *seeing*.

He quotes Thoreau, "We must look a long time before we can see … Nature will bear the closest inspection; she invites us to lay our eye level with the smallest leaf, and take an insect view of its plain."

Hardin went on to write:

> Seeing for Thoreau is more about a frame of mind
> than about photons impinging upon the retina.
> He has read the latest reports on horticulture,
> but he is frustrated that the farmer who witnesses
> the miracle of growth from seed to mature plant
> every day fails to apprehend the wonder of the
> process before him. For someone like myself,

immersed in … cellular processes in embryos,
Thoreau's attentiveness to the nature of nature is
an important reminder. Thoreau rekindled in me
a desire to inculcate in my own undergraduate
and graduate students a sense of the profundity of
creation amid the execution of their experimental
protocols.

At times the observant eyes of science and art meet, and the work of the poet Gerard Manley Hopkins illustrates this perfectly. He did something unusual, deliberately turning his back to the setting sun and examining the opposite skyline. He then wrote a letter to the scientific journal *Nature*, describing what he saw as "beams or spokes in the eastern sky about sunset, coming from a point due opposite the sun". This light effect is simply the shadows of clouds in front of the sun, cast from one horizon to the other, and it had already been observed by meteorologists. Perspective makes the shadows appear to be converging in the east, but they are in fact parallel. The technical name for them is anticrepuscular rays.

In 1881 *Nature* published a report saying that these rays had been seen in China, so Hopkins wrote in response. As a passionate observer of beauty, he exclaimed that "things common at home have sometimes first been remarked abroad", and "There seems no reason why the phenomenon should not be common, and perhaps if looked out for it would be found to be." He later wrote another letter to *Nature* reporting an especially strong set of anticrepuscular rays, caused (unbeknownst to him) by the eruption of a volcano on the Indonesian island of Krakatoa that sent ash clouds all over the world. The theologian and poet Chris Southgate calls this skill "intensive looking", and I'm sure there are many more examples of science being helped along by the eyewitness accounts of artists.

Unfortunately (or perhaps fortunately for hard-pressed editors), *Nature* no longer has a place for amateur writers. The scientific rigour of their letters section has risen since then, and it now contains mini scientific papers. Scientists themselves must look closely, though if they took the eye of a poet from time to time that might help them in their observations. As Hopkins said, "who looks east at sunset?"

Scientific beauty[130]

It should be obvious by now that the things scientists find beautiful are not always immediately attractive to the uninitiated beholder – though perhaps you can appreciate their enthusiasm. A scientist may find beauty in the objects they study – the data – whether that is a group of organisms, a diagnostic printout, or an aesthetically pleasing series of molecules. I've given some examples of this in biology, but chemists also enjoy this sort of beauty, as do astronomers. I'm sure that researchers in most fields of science find at least some of their data beautiful.

There is also the beauty of the cleverly devised experiment carried out with skill and patience. This is the sort of work that produces good clear results: the molecular biologist's sharp DNA bands on a gel, the organic chemist's high yield, or the physicist's precise measurements. When you focus hard on a technically demanding experiment and manage to complete it successfully, the outcome is a piece of work that is often very beautiful as well as useful. Colleagues gather round to admire your work, and requests begin to come in for you to teach others how to do the same techniques. Like most people, I didn't excel at every aspect of lab work but I managed to learn some techniques well, and I am still proud of a few nice pieces of data from my days as a PhD student. The best moment is when someone who has taught you says, "That's very nice!"

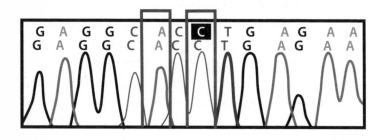

My nice "clean" DNA sequencing data

Another kind of beauty is introduced by the scientists themselves: perhaps some elegantly drawn graphs, or a carefully crafted presentation filled with photographs of microscopic organisms. Among my favourites at the moment are the black and white telescope images that are coloured to distinguish between different wavelengths of light, producing the most stunning images of stars and galaxies. This process of adding beauty to one's work is extremely satisfying, particularly if it helps your colleagues, friends, and family to appreciate why you spent all those days and nights in the lab.

Finally, there is a more abstract kind of beauty in science, and the first person to define this for me was a theologian. Jürgen Moltmann has been fascinated by science since he was a teenager, and when he gave a lecture at the Faraday Institute he mentioned beauty as an important part of the human side of science. According to Moltmann, beauty in science is seen most clearly when systems are moving from chaos to order, or vice versa. He is convinced that scientific beauty is not worth seeking for its own sake, but can be a sign that you are nearer the truth. Beauty may be useless from a utilitarian point of view, but it is meaningful in itself.[131]

Some of the best examples of this beauty in order come from physics. The theory – usually expressed as a mathematical equation – that gathers data into a coherent whole can have a beauty of its own that is both striking and satisfying. I find it hard to appreciate the beauty of equations, but when they show simplicity, symmetry, and unity, physicists call them beautiful. If a theory can be used to make predictions for further experiments and explain other types of data, then that adds to its beauty.[132]

I have found at least one example of beauty in mathematics that I can enjoy. Indian mathematicians first described a sequence of numbers, made famous in the West by Leonardo Fibonacci, where each new number is the sum of the previous two (1, 1, 2, 3, 5 and so on). This simple sum is useful in mathematics and computing, but also describes many repeating patterns found in nature. The arrangement of tree branches, leaves, flowers, and pinecones can all be described by Fibonacci numbers. So the abstract can also be beautiful, and some artists have copied nature, using this sequence to create stunning pictures.

A number of successful physicists have deliberately followed beauty in their search for truth, and Paul Dirac – winner of the Nobel Prize in 1933 – was one of these. He said that

> It was a sort of act of faith with us that any equations which describe fundamental laws of Nature must have great mathematical beauty in them ... It was a very profitable religion to hold and can be considered as the basis of much of our success.[133]

There was a flaw in Dirac's argument, however. Beauty can sometimes be an unreliable guide, and scientific revolutions have often involved a revolution in aesthetics. Einstein and a number of other physicists favoured continuity in their equations, so when quantum mechanics came along (a theory about the structure of the atom that involved electrons jumping from one energy level to another), it was difficult at first for the scientific community to accept it.[134] As the physicist Stephen Weinberg wrote, "... our sense of beauty is sometimes a useful guide and sometimes not..."[135]

This more abstract type of beauty is perhaps harder for a non-scientist to appreciate, but it is an important part of the scientific endeavour. Each of these very different types of scientific beauty involve characteristics that are intrinsic to the natural world, but they also require observation, imagination, and creativity on the part of the scientist. Through the work of scientists and artists like Jeff Hardin and Lizzie Burns, our eyes are continually being opened to new worlds of beauty.

Spirituality

So where does beauty take us? For some scientists, the beauty they see in their work points to something beyond science. These people are among the 20 per cent of elite researchers (see chapter one) who appreciate elements of spirituality but are not part of any particular faith community. Although my own convictions go further than this, I agree with these people that what we see in the lab points to something more than the measurements and pictures that make up our data.

The cell biologist Ursula Goodenough wrote in her book *The Sacred Depths of Nature* that

> the beauty of Nature – sunsets, woodlands,
> fireflies – has elicited religious emotions through
> the ages. We are moved to awe and wonder at
> the grandeur, the poetry, the richness of natural
> beauty; it fills us with joy and thanksgiving.

Although she rejects traditional religion, Goodenough gives time to thinking about what she calls "ultimate questions" because "the remarkable beauty of the cell, of everything that is, coupled with the improbability that life would have originated in the first place ... continues to draw me to spiritual issues". Like the mathematicians, she also thinks that beauty is an indicator of truth: "the creative scientist ... has as his or her goal the eureka, the unifying principle, the recognition of something beautiful embedded in Nature."

Werner Heisenberg, a physicist who worked on quantum mechanics, saw the beauty of these unifying principles as a gift. In 1925, at the age of twenty-three, he published his groundbreaking work on quantum mechanics. At the moment when everything came together and he was able to set out his theory, he felt such a high that he said it was like summiting a mountain. Not a believer in God, he described the beauty he saw in philosophical terms, saying that "Not even Plato could have believed that it would be so beautiful. In fact these relations cannot have been invented: they have existed since the creation of the world."[136]

Explaining his own experience of beauty in the lab, Jeff Hardin said, "I could talk about the theologian Rudolph Otto's 'sense of the numinous' – a spiritual feeling. But is there something more concrete than that? Is it, as the biblical scholar Tom Wright says, an 'echo of a voice'? I'd like to suggest to my colleagues that creation itself is calling out to us, saying something about its creator."

Christianity, science, and beauty

In saying that scientific beauty speaks of God, Hardin is drawing on a tradition that began over 2,000 years ago, and continues today. The Old Testament tells how the whole world speaks a message about the God who created everything. The Psalms say that "The heavens declare the glory of God; the skies proclaim the work of his hands" (Psalm 19), and "… the God of glory thunders, the Lord thunders over the mighty waters" (Psalm 29). The beauty of the land and everything in it is celebrated: mountains and trees, plants and animals, men and women.

The earliest Christian theologians, collectively called the

Church Fathers, often expressed their delight in the details of animal and plant life, and what we now understand as ecosystems. They were writing in the first to eighth centuries,[137] but their lack of scientific knowledge didn't stop them enjoying what they saw. The theologian Jame Schaefer has surveyed the writings of the Church Fathers, and also some medieval scholars. Many of them thought that a careful study of God's creation was essential to the serious worship of God. Their writing expresses great thankfulness that they are able to "read God's book of nature", unlike the foolish ones – they say – who pass all these delights by.

One of my favourites among the people Schaefer studied is an unnamed Cistercian monk from the twelfth century, who wrote about the grounds of the abbey in Clairvaux where he lived, and the surrounding countryside. He was obviously very happy with his vocation, and had a good understanding of the interconnectedness of the different factors: water, weather, and crops – an early ecology. He writes about the "friendly", "faithful", and "kindly stream" by the abbey and the different ways in which it serves the monks by providing for the fish, watering the plants and trees, helping things to grow in springtime, and filling up the lake.

Albert the Great lived a century later, and contributed to the early development of science. He wrote about how important it is to make observations and experiments, studying animals, plants, metals, and inorganic elements. He carried out field studies, and "legitimised the study of the natural world as a science within the Christian tradition". For him, the appreciation of creation involved both deep thinking and emotional sensitivity.

Schaefer noticed that these early theologians appreciated the beauty of creation on a number of different levels, starting on the surface and moving to a deeper, more intellectual understanding of both nature and God.[138] Her classification is interesting because it reflects the different reactions of scientists to what they see in their work today.

First, there is a simple delight in what is seen: an emotional appreciation that doesn't require any great thought or deep study. I can enjoy a tree just by looking at it, appreciating its colours and admiring the shape and pattern of its leaves and branches.

Second comes a more in-depth study. I could walk right up to the tree and touch its trunk, feeling the texture of the bark and noticing that it is covered with patches of lichen. I could look up and see the leaves stretching out in every direction to catch the sunlight, providing me with shade below. I could also find out what type of tree it is and learn some more details online. What sort of flowers or seeds does it have? How long will it live?

Third is a more abstract type of appreciation. I could think about other trees, and how their different species have come and gone over the millennia. Every organism is interconnected in some way: sharing air and water, decaying and becoming part of another organism. Each part plays its unique role in a global network of living things.

Fourth, and carrying on those more abstract ways of thinking, there is a feeling of mystery and incomprehensibility. There is something in the scale and complexity of the universe that eludes human comprehension. I could be struck by the absolutely vast number of these trees that exist, the billions of

seeds they scatter each year and the small fraction that su[n]
to maturity. It's difficult to take in, especially when I think of
how many other tree species there are, and what the world
might look like if all their seedlings survived.

Finally, these theologians appreciated a quality of the
world that could be called sacramental. For Christians,
visible things can remind us of the invisible God's presence
and character.[139] I could think about the fact that the tree has
stood on that spot for hundreds of years, and will probably
continue to do so long after I have died, which might remind
me of God's even greater strength and permanence. I will
explore this type of "natural theology" in more detail later in
the chapter.

So these early scholars believed that everyone should
study creation and enjoy its beauty using their God-given
intellect. Their detailed exploration of the wonders of the
universe was fuelled by faith in a benevolent creator God,
and their deep intellectual study led to heartfelt praise for the
one who made it.

God's philosophers[140]

As the modern practice of science began to emerge from the
sixteenth century onwards, science and faith were still tightly
meshed together. Natural philosophers – the early scientists
– continued the tradition of the Church Fathers, and carried
on using theological language in their work.

One of the most famous scientists of this period was
the astronomer Johannes Kepler. He had hoped to become a
theologian, but was unsuccessful. Eventually he realized that

science was also a way to serve God, and went on to make one of the most significant scientific discoveries of the seventeenth century: the laws of planetary motion. Kepler expressed his feelings about this in a letter to a friend, saying, "I wanted to become a theologian; for a long time I was unhappy. Now, behold, God is praised by my work, even in astronomy."[141] In another letter he wrote that "Nothing is greater and larger than the universe ... Nothing is more precious, nothing more beautiful."[142]

It was common (and sometimes compulsory) for academics during this period to be ordained clergy, and their science and theology were even more interwoven. So while Kepler was studying the planets, Reverend John Ray was a Fellow of Trinity College, Cambridge, and the author of the first textbook of modern botany. According to Ray, "There is for a free man no occupation more worthy and delightful than to contemplate the beauteous works of nature..."[143]

Later on, theological language was lost from scientific publications (a revolution that opened up science for people of all faiths, which can only be a good thing), but many scientists continued to celebrate the beauty of God's creation. Michael Faraday[144] was one of the nineteenth century's most prominent scientists, and is worth spending some time on, not least because the institute where I work is named after him. He is said to have been one of the greatest experimental scientists of all time but he shunned wealth and fame, and belonged to a small Christian denomination called the Sandemanians.

Faraday was the son of a blacksmith, received a very basic education as a child, and was apprenticed to a bookbinder at the age of fourteen. He was extremely bright, and a customer noticed his intelligence and gave him tickets to a series of lectures by the great chemist Humphrey Davy. Faraday was gripped. He wrote up his notes from the lectures and sent a bound copy to Davy, asking for a job. Davy was so impressed that he employed him as a secretary, and found him a job at the Royal Institution the following year. Faraday was appointed to the Royal Society[145] at the age of thirty-three, became director of the Royal Institution laboratory the following year, and Fullerian Professor of Chemistry at the same institute eight years later.

Though he worked long hours in the lab, Faraday managed to find time for other activities. He and his wife attended a marathon of church services on Sundays, with another gathering on Wednesday evenings. As a church elder he visited members in their homes and preached many sermons (sadly no records remain). He was also a great believer in public education, and he started the Royal Institute Friday Evening Discourses and the famous Christmas Lectures for children. He spoke in the plain style of a Sandemanian preacher, and drew huge audiences: both Charles Darwin and Charles Dickens attended his lectures.

Faraday was captivated by the beauty of science. In his children's talks on *The Chemical History of a Candle*, he called many things beautiful: the flames, shapes, air currents, and even the substance stearin (an ingredient of candle wax). In a letter to a colleague he remarked upon "The novelty and beauty of your new test for ozone",[146] and in one of his "Friday Discourse" lectures he said that

> The beauty of electricity or of any other force is
> not that the power is mysterious, and unexpected,
> touching every sense at unawares in turn, but that
> it is under *law*, and that the taught intellect can
> even now govern it largely.[147]

Faraday's main motivation for doing science was to glorify God by showing how incredible the world is. He was clearly a private man, and when his wife asked him why he chose to become a full member of the Sandemanian church after their marriage he said, "That is between me and my God."[148] He rejected a knighthood and the presidency of the Royal Society (twice) and Royal Institution, and turned down burial at Westminster Abbey. On his retirement, Faraday withdrew from the world of science and lived only two years. He died at the age of seventy-six and was buried without ceremony. His agnostic friend Sir John Tyndall described him as a "Just and faithful knight of God", and "the greatest experimental philosopher that the world has ever seen".[149]

Studying two books

Today, many scientists still see their work as a way to serve God and enjoy the beauty of what he has made. As a scientist, Jeff Hardin is walking in the footsteps of John Ray because he also has a degree in theology. He described to me how his approach to life in the lab takes both science and faith into account.

"There's the analogy of the 'two books', which comes from Psalm 19. There is the book of God's works in the world and there is also the book of God's word, which for Christians is the Bible. We need to take each of those books incredibly seriously. The regularity of heavenly bodies is the subject of discussion in Psalm 19, but there are other psalms that talk about biological processes, including predator-prey relationships. It's clear in these pieces of poetry that understanding those biological processes as well as you can is actually an exercise in giving glory to the one who stands behind them. To me that's part and parcel of being a scientist."

Jeff went on to say that "Christians, when they're doing science, are experiencing something that I call 'doxological fascination'. In other words they're locked in on a minute detail, as academics tend to do, and yet they're doing it for God's glory, in the same way that Johann Sebastian Bach wrote SDG, which is short for *Soli Deo Gloria* (glory to God alone), in all the margins of his manuscripts. They're trying to, as Johannes Kepler is reputed to have said, 'think God's thoughts after him'."

In a presentation to some Christian researchers, Jeff explained that "We need to be excited about biology as an act of worship. So in that sense, bringing glory, doxology, and fascination means being really fired up about what we are studying and being motivated to try to unlock the secrets of our research ... The creation is bubbling forth praise of the creator. That needs to be the bedrock upon which we do our biology." He finished by saying that "Whatever we ultimately choose to do ... I think God wants us to ... love doing our research. He wants it to seem like it's not fair that we should be paid to do it. I believe that's what he wants. The task for all of us is to ask the questions to help us get to that end point."

Natural theology

Going back to the "sacramental" side of creation, what would a theology of beauty look like? First, there is an aesthetics of theology itself. Karl Barth was a leading Protestant theologian of the last century, and he wrote that "theology ... is the most beautiful of all the sciences. To find the sciences distasteful is the mark of the Philistine. It is an extreme form of Philistinism to find ... theology distasteful."[150]

Moving to the person of God himself, there is a strong Christian tradition of studying what creation reveals about God – called natural theology. "[F]rom the beauty of the visible things let us form an idea of Him who is more than beautiful",[151] said Basil of Caesarea, one of the Church Fathers. Exploring this area of theology has helped me to understand what I experience when I see beauty in creation, either intuitively as I walk in a garden or wilderness area, or through the highly developed techniques of science or art.

Christians have generally approached natural theology in two ways, and one is more helpful than the other.[152] In the first, the beauty experienced in nature is just for starters – we must rise above it in order to reach God who is the perfect source of beauty. The beauty of creation is a pale, imperfect shadow of the beauty of God, so we mustn't dwell on it too much. This ascent from earthly to spiritual beauty is an idea from the Greek philosopher Plato that was adopted by some Christian theologians early in the history of the church.

The second way to view nature is that it is somehow transparent, so we can see God through it. In other words, we see the imprint of God's character in creation if we interpret it properly. This second, more horizontal concept has a more solid basis in the biblical idea of creation revealing God's glory. For example, Psalm 19:1 says that "The heavens declare the glory of God", Jesus uses nature parables to describe God, and the beginning of the book of Romans suggests that we can see something of God in creation.

The second way of seeing creation is also more challenging, because it requires discernment. There are several dangers Christians need to be aware of when trying to learn about God from what he has made. As Alister McGrath has said:

> If the heavens really are "telling the glory of God", this implies that something of God can be known through them ... But it does not automatically follow from this that *human beings*, situated as we are within nature, are capable unaided, or indeed capable under any conditions, of perceiving the divine through the natural order.[153]

First, creation is not God, so it does not fully reveal his character or purposes – for that we need Jesus. Second, as creation is not God, it is not to be worshipped or idolized in itself. Third, we are not perfect, so we need to be aware that we might deceive ourselves and say things about God's character that might be false. Finally, creation is described as "groaning" (Romans 8). The world we live in is not perfect and will only reveal God's character fully when it is renewed at the end of time (as described in Revelation 21).

For these reasons, some theologians – including Barth – have rejected natural theology entirely. Others have decided that, rather than throw the baby out with the bathwater, we should learn to discern what we can of God's attributes from creation.[154] God created the universe, so it bears marks of his character – however dimly perceived. Of course, every new insight should be tested thoroughly to see if it matches what is written in the Bible, and kept firmly in the context of the Christian message of hope.

Alister McGrath put it this way: "The Christian doctrine of creation provides an intellectual framework for seeing God *through* nature…"[155] He goes on to say that the birth of Jesus allows us to see God's physical presence in nature: a culmination of everything he has made. I think this second approach makes sense. Many Christians intuitively experience creation as an important point of contact with God, so why not tap into that tendency and learn to use it well?

Beauty and the character of God

So what *does* the beauty of creation reveal about God? When I get to this point, I often start to struggle. How can we even begin to describe the creator of the universe? I found one theologian, Karl Rahner, helpful on this point.[156] He said that studying God is a balancing act. At times the theologian has to hold their breath, as it were, and suspend their sense of the sacred in order to understand deep truths. But they should also keep their connection with spiritual experience. This is "theology on its knees" in worship. Emotion, beauty, and art are all important to help keep this balance.[157]

I feel the same as Rahner about conversations on science and theology. It's fascinating to look at examples of how the universe looks finely tuned for life, because perhaps this is a pointer to the existence of God. Logical analysis of the physical constants involved requires a good deal of spiritual breath-holding, but it's possible – at least for a time – to remain focused on the physics. It's when I look at what creation reveals of God's character that I begin to find it difficult to sit still and calmly rational in the library. I will hold my breath for now, but I will finish with some reflections on worship in the chapter on awe.

One of the main theologians to deal with beauty in recent decades was the Catholic scholar Hans Urs von Balthasar. He was upset that aesthetics had been established as its own academic field, because separating beauty from logic (truth) and ethics (goodness) meant that art was then seen as a product to be consumed, and no longer useful for the life of the mind. He redressed the balance with his multivolume work *The Glory of the Lord*, which focused on theological aesthetics.

A number of people, including Jeff Hardin, suggested to me that I should explore Balthasar's work because he has almost singlehandedly reinstated beauty as a subject that theologians – both Protestant and Catholic – should be discussing. So after reading a commentary on Balthasar[158] (his books are famously difficult to understand) and a number of other theologians, I have gleaned three main ways in which beauty can show us something about God's character.

First, the beauty of the world is a reflection of the beauty of God.[159] Psalm 27 contains a very moving expression of this: "One thing I ask from the Lord, this only do I seek: that I may dwell in the house of the Lord all the days of my life, to gaze on the beauty of the Lord and to seek him in his temple." The beauty of God is expressed in his holiness and majesty, his deep love for people, his justice, forgiveness and generosity – and the list could go on for a long time. The writer of this psalm has managed to ignore other distractions and focus on God's beauty for a time, and that's a very special place to be. What does the beauty of God mean? Perhaps the next best word is "glory" – one that has already been used a good deal in this chapter. I could use other words to replace this rather old-fashioned word: grandeur, greatness, splendour, magnificence, majesty, brilliance – but glory is useful because it sums them all up in a single word.

This aspect of natural theology was important for Augustine of Hippo. He was a grown man before he began to appreciate the beauty of his surroundings, and he wanted to find the source of that beauty. Through his search he found God. In his book *Confessions*, he wrote that his love for the beauty of the world now reflected his love for God. Later in life, he wrote that every part of creation helped him to appreciate God's beauty, and "If I were to take each one of them individually, and unwrap them, as it were, and examine them, along with all the rich blessings contained within them, how long it would take!"[160]

Writing nearly one and a half thousand years later, Barth thought beauty was an absolutely essential part of God's glory, but he didn't want people to focus on it because he was worried about nature-worship. Balthasar was less cautious, and said that the beauty of creation reflects God's glory, because that is its purpose. "For the glory of God the world was created", said Balthasar, and that has implications for the life of a Christian: "... only the person who is touched by a ray of this glory ... can learn to see the presence of [God] in Jesus Christ."[161]

The second way in which science shows something of God is the order and interconnectedness of the world. This was an important point for many of the early theologians, who saw God's power, wisdom, and goodness in creation. The medieval scholar Thomas Aquinas wrote that "Each creature manifests God in some way, but the best manifestation of God is the beautifully ordered universe of all creatures functioning in relation to one another as God intended."[162] Basil of Caesarea put it more poetically, saying that "The world is a work of art, set before all for contemplation, so that through it the wisdom of Him who created it should be known."[163]

The grand picture of the world painted by science today is even more dynamic and interconnected than these early theologians could have imagined: many animals, plants, and microbes interacting together; an environment where seismic events and thermal cycles combine to create varied ecological niches; a planet with lunar and solar systems that provide tides and seasons, and a universe where immense physical forces create the stability needed for that planet to exist. God has endowed the world with properties that enable things to "create themselves", and without his generosity, patience, and sustaining power, nothing would exist at all.

Finally, and entering the realm of the physicists, the beauty of the world also shows something of God at a more abstract level. The first chapter of Genesis and the first chapter of John describe a God who creates order out of chaos. The symmetry, pattern, and intricate detail we see in nature are the result of finely balanced physical properties. A snowflake is symmetrical because the laws underlying its formation are symmetrical.[164] The order and fine-tuning in the universe still prompt some astronomers to ask questions about God, and as I mentioned at the end of chapter five, similar-sounding arguments are beginning to emerge among biologists and earth scientists.

Hinting

Some have spoken of beauty as evidence for God, but I prefer to think of it as a thought experiment. If a good God created a world, what would you expect? I would expect great beauty. And if we are created in God's image, it is perhaps not surprising that we are equipped to appreciate the beauty we see.

The physicist Subrahmanyan Chandrasekhar has put forward the idea that scientists who are more aesthetically aware are more likely to do great work. In a more recent paper Tracee Hackel, a pastor and theologian, has suggested that Christians are necessarily more aware of the beauty of God, so more likely to notice the beauty of creation. Or would people who are more attuned to the beauty of creation be more likely to recognize the beauty of God? I'm not sure which applies, but Augustine's quest for beauty shows that what we see in nature can lead some people to God, no matter how circuitous the route.

Jeff Hardin put it this way: "Science for a Christian is, in some very real sense, an exercise in art appreciation, and art historians must take works of art on their own terms and try to understand them. The theologian Hans Urs von Balthasar has written a good deal about aesthetics, and how it feeds into epistemology (how we know what we know), and even to metaphysics [the fundamental nature of things – including philosophy and religion]. I'm trying to explore that in my own thinking and reading. For me, being a Christian means that I need to take the world as it is and understand it as well as I can, in the same way that someone who's studying a work of art must take it as it is and try to understand it for its own sake, as well as he or she can."

I agree with Jeff, and with Augustine when he says that beauty points to God, but I take Augustine's argument in a more general way. In fact, I would say it even more cautiously – that beauty hints at God's presence. This passage from Augustine's commentary on Psalm 26 is a wonderful example of his writing on this subject. It speaks to me of how beauty is the first step in wondering where that beauty comes from – and for a Christian, it can remind us very strongly of God.

> Let your mind roam through the whole creation;
> everywhere the created world will cry out to
> you: "God made me". Whatever pleases you in
> a work of art brings to your mind the artist who
> wrought it; much more, when you survey the
> universe, does the consideration of it evoke praise
> for its Maker. You look on the heavens; they are
> God's great work. You behold the earth; God
> made its numbers of seeds, its varieties of plants,
> its multitudes of animals. Go round the heavens
> again and back to the earth, leave out nothing; on

all sides everything cries out to you of its Author;
nay the very forms of created things are as it were
the voices with which they praise their creator.[165]

Conclusion: The weight of glory

Scientists enjoy beauty in the same way that we enjoy the
serenity of a garden or carefully tended olive grove on a
summer's day. Bringing order from chaos, watching things
develop and become chaotic again and bringing order once
more using reason, creativity, and imagination, is one of the
most fulfilling experiences in life. The startling elegance of
the mathematical solution, or the model that makes sense
of what seemed to be a muddle of data is the beauty of
shalom[166] (a Hebrew word whose definition includes peace,
contentment, welfare, and completeness). Not only is the
prospect attractive, but it is also deeply satisfying, ordered,
and harmonious.

To achieve that state the scientist, gardener, or farmer
has expended time and energy. The process can be protracted,
complicated, expensive, and at times painful, but somehow
we have the drive to do it over and over again. To me, the
Christian teaching that God has made us in his image, and
often uses long and complex processes in order to work out
his plans in the world, makes perfect sense of that experience.

C. S. Lewis thought that our experience of beauty was
a taste of something to come, and he wrote about this in his
essay *The Weight of Glory*. If we are fascinated by what we see
in creation and find it beautiful, and if it awakens something
in us that we can't put a name to, Lewis would say that we

have a "desire for our own far-off country".[167] He wrote that we are longing "for something that has never actually appeared in our experience", but everything we see hints at it.

No matter what we do to tame that desire by giving it the name "beauty", the feeling just won't go away. We want everything to be beautiful and ordered, but it isn't. The beauty of creation awakens something in us, and we want to find its source. If we try to satisfy ourselves with the beauty of what we see around us, Lewis said:

> The books or the music [or science] in which we thought the beauty was located will betray us if we trust to them; it was not *in* them, it only came *through* them, and what came through them was longing … For they are not the thing in itself; they are only the scent of a flower we have not found, the echo of a tune we have not heard, news from a country we have never yet visited.

For Lewis, what we are longing for is the "new heaven and … new earth" that are promised in the symbolic account of the end of time in Revelation (chapters 21 and 22). "We cannot mingle with the splendours we see. But all the leaves of the New Testament are rustling with the rumour that it will not always be so. Some day, God willing, we shall get *in*."

So my response to the beauty I see in nature is to enjoy it, to be grateful for it, and to allow it to remind me of God. The great cathedrals are a human expression of the beauty of nature, with pillars, colourful windows, and tiny details in stone, designed to remind us of God's greatness and creative power. I appreciate these wonderful spaces, but I prefer to see the original – I'd rather be in a forest.

To appreciate creation to the full, Schaefer suggests seeking out information about what we are looking at – which a scientist will need no encouragement to do – and being open to new experiences, reflecting those back to God. Opening ourselves up to surprise, fascination, and curiosity helps to foster an awareness of the bigger reality that includes both ourselves and the rest of creation. For scientists like Jeff Hardin and myself, the beauty we see in creation reminds us of God and moves us to both wonder and worship.

Chapter 7

Wonder

The most amazing thing about mammalian development is … that it ever succeeds.
Veronica van Heyningen, geneticist[168]

Reality is always more surprising than we are capable of imagining.
Jürgen Moltmann, theologian[169]

Believe it or not, studying little stripy fish is a great way to understand processes that are important to human health. Like many of the organisms that biologists study, zebrafish are popular for fairly mundane reasons. They are cheap to look after, have a short life cycle, lay large quantities of eggs, and can be bought from any pet shop. Most importantly, the anatomy and chemistry of their bodies is similar to our own. Zebrafish have helped us to understand a number of human diseases, including heart defects and muscle-wasting disorders. They are also surprisingly beautiful close up.

I'll never forget my first encounter with zebrafish. I was interviewing for a PhD scholarship, and my future supervisor was showing me around the lab. When she took me to the fish room I was surprised to see that zebrafish don't actually look like their namesakes, because their stripes run horizontally.

The adults shimmered and darted around the tanks, and some had spots instead of stripes, or long trailing fins. I could see why these fish are popular aquarium pets, but it was their offspring that had me transfixed.

When I looked down a microscope at a dish of wiggling zebrafish larvae, I was – as Jeff Hardin said when he saw his first sea urchin embryo – absolutely hooked. At twenty-four hours old, they are about two and a half millimetres long and almost completely translucent. I could see every detail of their anatomy in minute detail. I could see their hearts pumping, and tiny red blood cells moving through their blood vessels. I could trace the outline of muscle fibres in their tails, and see every detail of their developing eyes. Later on the eye becomes covered in silvery pigment cells, the transparent lens protruding, beautifully rounded and greenish in colour. I was full of questions, and wanted to get to work immediately. I was excited to have three whole years to learn about these beautiful organisms, and I never grew tired of looking at them.

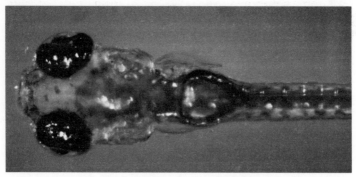

A four-day-old zebrafish larva, viewed from above

Everyone in the lab feels a sense of wonder from time to time. Maybe they see something new in an experiment that sparks their curiosity, or they might find a surprising result when they analyse a collection of data. Maybe they just have a few spare minutes to stare at the things they study and become lost in fascination. Each person will come to a different conclusion about what they see and what it points to, but wonder seems to be part of the package in science. It is an experience that raises spiritual questions for some, and enhances faith for others.

Wonderful cells

My scientist of faith for this chapter is Rhoda Hawkins, a theoretical physicist and lecturer at the University of Sheffield. Rhoda uses physics to tackle biological problems, and the main focus of her research at the moment is the properties of cells and how they move. She and her students use mathematical or computer models to make predictions, and they collaborate with lab-based researchers (mainly biologists and other physicists) who test those predictions. The long-term aim of their work is to understand more about the immune system and the movement of cells in cancer.

It was fascinating to hear Rhoda using the language of physics to explain something biological. I was reminded that even the simplest-looking organism is incredibly complex on the inside. Her description of a cell was, "It's not a solid and it's not a liquid; it's somewhere in between the two. 'Squidgy' is a good word to describe it.

"We use theories that have been developed for squidgy materials, and then we think about the fact that this is a material that's alive, and how that makes it different. In physics language it's called 'out of equilibrium', which means there's an internal source of energy from the food that the cell or the organism is eating. It uses that energy to exert forces and move in a way that a non-living material wouldn't. You wouldn't expect a blob of hair gel to start crawling across your shower floor unless you pushed it – whereas a cell, which has a similar consistency, is able to move on its own."

When I asked Rhoda what motivated her to work on such difficult problems, she returned to the properties of the cell. "I find cell movement incredible. You've got a blob of squidgy material and it's crawling across a surface or it's squeezing through a gap. If it's a white blood cell it might be doing something more complicated like chasing a bacterium. I look at that and I just ask, 'Why? How is it capable of doing that when it's a relatively simple thing?'"

For Rhoda, wonder is "that thing that makes you say, 'Wow'. There's an amazement about it that goes beyond what you've done yourself. So it's, 'Wow, this works! We've started with these equations and we've got an answer that makes sense and fits with the experimental data.' It's an acknowledgment of beauty in the system and amazement at the world around us."

Of course, every researcher does not bounce out of bed every day anticipating the wonders they will see. Rhoda finds that her sense of wonder is renewed when she interacts with her colleagues. "If I haven't been to a conference for several months I can find myself getting a little bit dry. I'll be looking forward to the next opportunity to listen to somebody talking about their work, because that fires me up again. It gets you out of the details that you're bogged down in and provides you with a bigger picture. I'm amazed by what they've done, and I find that inspirational for my own work, even if it's not directly relevant."

So, like beauty, wonder is another force that drives scientific research. "I see a mountain and I want to climb up it," said Rhoda. "It could be really tough to get up there, and you could be tired – but then when you get to the top you've got this amazing view, and a sense of satisfaction and achievement. So even the struggle is contributing to that sense of wonder. If climbing the mountain was too easy, then you wouldn't feel so happy when you got to the top."

Awe and wonder[170]

I have found that many people use the words "awe" and "wonder" interchangeably, but they don't mean exactly the same thing. Wonder is a stepping stone on the way to awe, so I'll need to define awe first.

Awe is the mixture of overwhelmment, wonder, and fear that we feel when we come across things that are larger, more beautiful, more powerful or complex than anything we see in our everyday lives. To be awestruck is one of the most basic human experiences. The night sky, vast landscapes or the mighty forces of wind and sea are accessible to almost every person on earth, and can affect us deeply. Architecture, paintings, and music often move us in a similar way. Awe invokes feelings of reverence or respect. There is also the need for mental adjustment or accommodation: before we can take it in we need to make room in our mental map of the world for this new and amazing thing.[171]

Wonder on its own – what you might call childlike wonder – is what we experience when we're confronted by anything new or unexpected. Wonder is an active and hopeful feeling, because we have the opportunity to learn when we come up against the unfamiliar. We are amazed and surprised, and it makes us curious. We want to examine and understand it. We might begin to doubt what we thought we knew about it, and enjoy the process of asking questions and beginning to untangle its mysteries. There may also be an element of mental adjustment as we try to make sense of it. Overall, to wonder is a pleasant experience because the object of our attention is fascinating but not threatening.

What I have given so far is the standard dictionary definition of wonder, but like beauty, there have been different uses of the word throughout Western history. We have arrived at a point where wonder is seen to be a positive emotion or activity, but it could easily have been otherwise. For the ancient Greek philosophers, wonder was the root of learning because coming up against the unknown makes us look for answers. The early scientists (in the sixteenth and seventeenth centuries) continued in this tradition, and the great philosophers of science, Francis Bacon and René Descartes, saw wonder as an opportunity to increase knowledge.

As the seventeenth century drew to a close and the Age of Enlightenment was born,[172] wonder began to be seen in a negative light, and was associated with ignorance and superstition. The Enlightenment philosopher Adam Smith described wonder as a disturbing emotion that must be dispelled with knowledge. When we come across something new, he wrote, it throws us outside of our usual categories of thinking and we must investigate it until we find a connection with something more familiar. Once we have found a mental pigeonhole for the offending item, peace is restored.

Smith thought the urge to eliminate wonder was a driving force in the development of modern science. But when Romanticism began to emerge towards the end of the eighteenth century, imagination and emotion came to the fore, and wonder and awe were back in vogue. Wonder is a way to "reclaim a lost childhood", and has been taken seriously by a number of philosophers.[173]

Today, in a sense, we have returned to our roots. Children are encouraged to be wonderers and adults try to keep their sense of wonder alive. A writer wonders about the meaning of a word, and a chef wonders about the flavour of a new ingredient. A gardener wonders why roses grow so well in certain types of soil, and a scientist wonders how physical forces can work together to produce something so strange and beautiful. Once again, wonder is the root of knowledge.

Cultivating wonder

If wonder is so important, how can we cultivate it? Like beauty, the experience of wonder will only come to us if we pay attention. "The world will never starve for want of wonders; but only for want of wonder." A colleague sent me this quote, and when I followed up its source I discovered that it was from a short story called "Tremendous Trifles" by

G. K. Chesterton, the writer and critic whose *Father Brown* detective stories I enjoyed as a teenager.

Chesterton's story is of two boys – Peter and Paul – playing in a tiny, boring, suburban garden consisting of "four strips of gravel, a square of turf with some mysterious pieces of cork standing up in the middle and one flower bed with a row of red daisies". A fairy passes by in the guise of a milkman and offers the boys each a wish.

Paul chooses to become a giant, roams the planet in a few strides, and finds that the world is not as exciting as he had hoped: "… when he came to the Himalayas, he found they were quite small and silly-looking, like the little cork rockery in the garden…" He gets bored, lies down on a prairie for a nap, and has his head chopped off by a woodcutter. Chesterton was obviously writing more in the tradition of Brothers Grimm than Disney.

Peter wishes differently, and chooses to become very small. He is immediately plunged down into a vast landscape full of exciting new sights to explore.

> … he found himself in the midst of an immense plain, covered with a tall green jungle and above which, at intervals, rose strange trees each with a head like the sun in symbolic pictures, with gigantic rays of silver and a huge heart of gold … far away on the faint horizon he could see the line of another forest, taller and yet more mystical, of a terrible crimson colour, like a forest on fire for ever.

The world Peter saw was familiar, but more exciting than anything he had seen before. "He set out on his adventures across that coloured plain; and he has not come to the end of it yet."

The aim of Chesterton's story was to "show how many extraordinary things even a lazy and ordinary man may see if he can spur himself to the single activity of seeing". Whether one's inability to climb mountains or travel to far-flung places comes from indolence (like Chesterton) or lack of resources, "we may, by fixing our attention almost fiercely on the facts actually before us, force them to turn into adventures; force them to give up their meaning and fulfil their mysterious purpose…" A world of wonders awaits the observant individual.

> Everything is in an attitude of mind … I will
> sit still and let the marvels and the adventures
> settle on me like flies. There are plenty of them, I
> assure you. The world will never starve for want of
> wonders; but only for want of wonder.

Perhaps it is no accident that the characters in Chesterton's story were young. Children are experts in wonder because they're constantly encountering things for the first time. They have no choice but to be open to the world and what it has to show them. In his book *Unweaving the Rainbow*, Richard Dawkins reminds us how easy it is to lose our sense of wonder as adults. "There is an anaesthetic of familiarity, a sedative of ordinariness, which dulls the senses and hides the wonder of existence."[174]

Science, says Dawkins, opens our eyes to everyday wonders.

> … it is at least worthwhile from time to time making an effort to shake off the anaesthetic. What is the best way of countering the sluggish habituation brought about by our gradual crawl from babyhood? We can't actually fly to another planet. But we can recapture that sense of having just tumbled out to life on a new world by looking at our own world in unfamiliar ways.[175]

If, like Chesterton, we choose not to move far, we can find some examples of these scientific wonders in our own bodies. Until recently I believed we had enough DNA in our bodies to take us on an amazing journey. I was told that if every chromosome in every cell of my body was extracted and added end-to-end they would reach to the moon and back. That's quite a thought. But when I checked the numbers I discovered the story I had been told was way off the mark.

We have about 50 trillion cells in our bodies. Multiply that by two, and you have about 100 trillion metres, or 100 billion kilometres of DNA. The distance to the moon is about 380,000 kilometres. If you do the maths, you'll find that we do have enough DNA in our bodies to take us to the moon and back, but there's a lot left over. The distance to the sun is about 150 million kilometres, so the DNA in the average human body could take you to the sun and back more than 300 times.[176] Does that begin to "lift the anaesthetic's pall"?

Questions

For Rhoda Hawkins, the main pleasure of wondering is in the questions she gets to ask. "Some people can look at a rainbow and just say, 'Oh, that's beautiful.' That's great, but I can't stop there; I want to know why it's beautiful. Sometimes as a child, adults get frustrated with you when you keep asking 'Why?', and effectively tell you to shut up. Scientists are the people who are still allowed to ask those questions."

Scientists have to come up with original questions, and that is another reason why Rhoda has been drawn to working at the interface between physics and biology. Traditionally, there have been quite clear boundaries between different subjects in science. In the past, said Rhoda, "physicists have said, 'Oh no, that's biology, that's not me, and therefore I won't touch it', and biologists have said, 'Oh no, that's forces and physics, and that's not me, I won't touch it'." Rhoda has chosen to apply her skills in physics to biological questions, because "there are a lot of interesting questions on the edge of these subjects that have not been addressed".

Rhoda said that her passion to ask questions sometimes gets the better of her, but she wouldn't have it any other way. "Sometimes, I've got stuck in projects I've been working on where the question I'm asking is too difficult, or beyond where we are at the moment, and we just can't answer it. That's really frustrating, and yet grappling with that is better than not having asked the question in the first place. If you're not allowed to ask the questions, it's stifling."

Having said that wonder can be like climbing a mountain, Rhoda used another metaphor that expressed her enjoyment of science. "It's like opening a door in a big building or a castle, and realizing that there are more rooms than you thought. By doing this piece of research you've opened up a door into other questions and other areas that you didn't even know were there before." This is a very attractive picture of science, but is that all there is to it?

Deeper wonder

Adam Smith thought learning drives out wonder, and to some extent he's right. A certain kind of wonder can sometimes be lost in the process of taking things apart. The poet Keats expressed this in his poem "Lamia", saying that scientists "unweave a rainbow", and, "Do not all charms fly at the mere touch of cold philosophy?"

I experienced this disillusionment myself as a child. I remember wondering how my food and drink knew where to go in my body when I swallowed them, in order for their waste products to exit neatly from different places. I think I had imagined some sort of complex series of pipes. My parents were both doctors, and they explained – in their usual matter-of-fact way – that food and drink are swallowed down the same "tube", mixed up in my stomach and separated later. This answer wasn't nearly exciting enough for my childish imagination, so I lost interest in any further explanation.

If science causes some to lose their sense of wonder, then how do people like Rhoda keep going? I learned the answer to this question from a science teacher. The Danish historian of science Olaf Pedersen began his working life in the classroom, and he discovered the wonder of scientific discovery through teaching two physics lessons.

In the first, rather unsuccessful, lesson, he followed the textbook. He described the specific gravity (a measure of density) of lead to a group of eleven-year-olds, and then gave them pieces of lead to weigh and measure. The class started their work enthusiastically, but obviously school rulers weren't up to the task, and they failed to come up with the exact figure for the specific gravity of lead that was given in the book. They became discouraged, and lost interest.

Pedersen realized that to make his lessons more interesting he needed to turn them upside down. The next year he began by giving out pieces of lead and asking his students to weigh and measure them. They entered their results in a table on the blackboard, and started doing calculations. They multiplied, added and subtracted the numbers in the columns, but all they got was nonsense. Eventually they tried dividing mass by volume and started getting a remarkably similar number for each different sample of lead. The children were fascinated and began to ask questions, which provided the perfect window of opportunity for Pedersen to explain the concept of specific gravity.

Of course, Pedersen's class knew they could have found the figure they "discovered" by looking it up in a textbook, but their fascination was not about original discovery. Neither was it about getting the right answer. They were excited because they had found something that had been previously hidden to them.

Rhoda Hawkins has had the same experience as Pedersen with her own students. "I love seeing the light dawning as they understand something for the first time. I can see it on their faces, even if they don't say anything. Sometimes they express themselves in a way that shows they're experiencing that wonder and amazement at understanding how something works. For me, that's one of the reasons why I enjoy teaching."

The philosopher and cognitive scientist Margaret Boden described this sense of deepening wonder as a journey from ignorant to informed wonder.[177] She tells the story of a colleague who was fascinated by circles as a young child. He collected all sorts of round objects, kept them in a cupboard, and used them as templates for drawing circles. His parents noticed his new hobby and decided to encourage it. They promised him an instrument that could draw circles of any size. Imagining some sort of magical expanding object, he was filled with wonder and excitement and could hardly wait to receive his gift.

On the day the circle-making machine appeared, the boy's dreams were shattered. The compass he was given was not at all what he had been expecting. It was so simple and boring, and not at all circular. It completely destroyed his love of circles. Boden's colleague felt such a strong feeling of disillusionment at the time that he remembered it as a "traumatic event in his childhood". I expect his parents felt terrible too.

All too familiar – a compass

As an adult mathematician, however, Boden's colleague learned to appreciate the elegant simplicity of the compass. Now he understands the mathematical principle behind it, he can see that this instrument is indeed a wonderful thing. Deeper understanding led to deeper wonder. As Boden writes, "When wonder is based on pure ignorance or on error and illusion, it must fade in the light of understanding … But understanding may lead in turn to a new form of wonder, which cannot be so easily destroyed."

I wondered if this obsession with wonder was a purely Western phenomenon, so I emailed a Chinese friend: a mathematician who works on circles. Does he experience the deeper, informed wonder that comes with knowledge? It turns out that he does. He explained how as a high school student he was fascinated by Pascal's Theorem, which is to do with the geometry of circles. He thought it was beautiful, though he didn't completely understand it. But as a graduate student studying advanced mathematics, he came to appreciate Pascal's work more fully, and found it even more wonderful than before. He said, "There are many such wonders in mathematics, which have been serving as a motivation for my study. I am on my way to discover more such deep wonders!"

Thankfully, I never completely lost my own curiosity about that system of pipes. When I studied biology at university I learned about the exquisite detail and complex biochemistry of the gut, liver, and kidney, and my sense of wonder at the human body returned. The more I find out about the living world, the more my amazement grows.

The gift of wonder

Einstein thought the most surprising and fascinating thing about the natural world is that we can make sense of it: "… the eternal mystery of the world is its comprehensibility".[178] Like Pedersen's pupils, a scientist might start with a jumble of data, but after some patient sorting and calculating they notice a pattern – maybe a potential mathematical description or a link between one process and another. To discover that pattern for yourself is stunning. It was there all along, just waiting to be found.

Rhoda feels this sense of amazement from time to time in her own work. "What gives me an enormous sense of wonder is when I do a calculation and it works. That does not happen often! Usually I've proved the equivalent of one equals two or something else that's very wrong, or I've just gone around in a big circle and proved that zero equals zero. Every now and then you solve a calculation and get an answer which makes sense. I find it amazing that we can use the language of mathematics and our finite human brains to understand something in the physical universe."

At times, wrote Pedersen, a scientist who has gone through the process of discovering and making sense of things might feel as if they have invented something. On a more fundamental level though, they have done nothing of the sort. The language used by many people when they describe the moment of breakthrough is that they have found a reality that was always there. The physicist Heisenberg wrote:

> when one stumbles upon these very simple, great
> connections … the whole thing appears in a
> different light. Then our inner eye is suddenly
> opened to a connection which has always been
> there – also without us – and which is quite
> obviously not created by man.[179]

Biologists can also have this experience. In *The Sense of Wonder*, the marine biologist and writer Rachel Carson describes the adventures she had exploring nature with her young nephew.

She asks:

> What is the value of preserving and strengthening
> this sense of awe and wonder, this recognition
> of something beyond the boundaries of human
> existence? Is the exploration of the natural world
> just a pleasant way to pass the golden hours of
> childhood or is there something deeper?

She then answers her own question, saying:

> I am sure there is something much deeper,
> something lasting and significant. Those who
> dwell, as scientists or laymen, among the beauties
> and mysteries of the earth are never alone or
> weary of life ... There is symbolic as well as actual
> beauty in the migration of the birds, the ebb and
> flow of the tides, the folded bud ready for spring.

So where does deeper wonder take you? Pedersen noticed that the experience of discovery is sometimes so powerful that scientists say they feel as if they have received a gift. The Nobel prize-winning particle physicist Carlo Rubbia described his own feelings of gratitude and wonder in a public lecture:

> When we look at a particular physical
> phenomenon, for example a starry night, we feel
> deeply moved; we feel within ourselves a message
> which comes from nature, which transcends it
> and dominates it ... The beauty of nature, seen

from within and in its most essential terms, is
even more perfect than what appears externally ...
I feel curiosity and am honoured to be able to see
these things, fortunate, because nature is in fact a
spectacle that is never exhausted.[180]

A gift implies a giver, and though Pedersen is reluctant to take it further, the theological connection has been made. A deep sense of wonder is not evidence for God, but it might get us thinking beyond what we can see in front of our noses. Neither Heisenberg nor Einstein believed in God,[181] but they both believed that there is a reality beyond science, and they used spiritual language to describe it. If they were alive, they would belong to Ecklund's "spiritual but not religious group" of scientists.[182]

Faith, science, and wonder

For a scientist who is also a Christian, the wonder they feel at work can have a very positive impact on their faith. One person who has experienced this is John Bryant, Emeritus Professor of Cell and Molecular Biology at Exeter University and former chair of Christians in Science. He described to me the moment of discovery, when something new and exciting is shared between you and only one or two other people"

Being, for a short time, one of just a handful of
people ... who know that information is a real
privilege. I'm not going to deny that an atheist
feels awe and wonder, because they do. I think

that is just increased when you realize that these
intricate mechanisms you're seeing are the work of
an awesome creator.

John explained how he appreciates those "moments of
awareness ... that may remind us of the wonder of the
creation and the awesomeness of the creator". For him,
this is a moment of being "especially aware of the spiritual
dimension of our existence, even being particularly conscious
of the presence of God or perhaps having an enhanced sense
of his glory". It is "a deeper feeling of wonder at the fact that
he who put the code in DNA invites us to call him Father".[183]

Does this sense of spiritual closeness disappear on a more
in-depth study of God, or is it like science, where a more
lasting wonder develops? I found three theologians who have
considered wonder in this context, and all of them have a
very strong scientific background. Their different insights
have helped me to appreciate the concept of deeper wonder
in a Christian context.

First comes the theologian Alister McGrath, who also has
a PhD in biophysics. McGrath has described three ways in
which we can experience wonder at nature, which are similar
to Jame Schaefer's five ways of appreciating beauty (in chapter
six) and they provide a good summary of the different types
of wonder I have been describing in the last two sections.[184]

First, there is the sense of "immediate wonder" that we
can all experience in response to natural beauty. This type
of wonder doesn't require any special knowledge, there is no
theoretical reflection, and no philosophizing. This is pure
perception, before any thinking happens. I felt immediate

wonder when I saw my first zebrafish larvae, and Rhoda feels it when she sees cell movement.

Next, if immediate wonder leads to scientific exploration, we have the privilege of experiencing even more wonder as we see how incredible it all is: more highly organized and even more beautiful than it seemed at first. This "derived wonder" at the elegant simplicity of mathematical or theoretical representations of reality is the deeper or informed wonder that Pedersen's pupils, Boden's colleague, and many others have experienced. This is also Dawkins' religion, if he has one. In *Unweaving the Rainbow* he wrote:

> The feeling of awed wonder that science can give us is one of the highest experiences of which the human psyche is capable. It is a deep aesthetic passion to rank with the finest that music and poetry can deliver. It is truly one of the things that makes life worth living ...[185]

McGrath's final type of wonder is spiritual or theological. It is another kind of derived wonder, provoked by "what the natural world points to".[186] As I mentioned in the last chapter, the beauty of creation can point to its creator, and wonder is also part of that experience. I felt this sense of spiritual wonder when I read another book by Richard Dawkins called *River Out of Eden*. Dawkins is a past master at building up a description of a biological process, starting with the earliest research and adding layer upon layer until it is fully explained. I remember reading his passage on the dance of the honeybee and thinking, "God, you made those things! They're amazing!" My picture of God had expanded. He sustained the long and patient process of evolution, and he also communicates with me.

The next wondering theologian is Celia Deane-Drummond, who began her career as a lecturer in plant science, and is now Professor of Theology at the University of Notre Dame in the USA. Deane-Drummond thinks that wonder drives us to learn and develop wisdom because it marks out the limits of our own understanding. Discovering something intriguing prompts us to find out more, leading to wisdom or knowledge. Wonder can also lead us to other realities, because intense scientific or philosophical enquiry may show the limits of what is natural or material. This prompts people to ask more philosophical questions.[187]

Ultimately, says Deane-Drummond, wonder informed by wisdom can lead to spiritual exploration. The question is, does scientific wonder actually point to God? The answer is yes, but not very far. Einstein and Heisenberg had a sense of something "out there", but their scientific exploration didn't take them any further. As I said in the last chapter, creation isn't God – it just reflects something of his character. So there are limits to the number of places that a journey from science to religion can take you, but it can be a very good starting point for a fruitful discussion.[188]

Last but not least, is a theologian who had a long and distinguished career in science. John Polkinghorne was a particle physicist and Professor of Mathematical Physics at Cambridge University, before becoming ordained in the Anglican Church. So Polkinghorne is well acquainted with the deeper sense of wonder that comes through an in-depth study of science and, like Drummond, he thinks the most coherent explanation for this is God. He is amazed that our minds and the tools we use in science are capable of making sense of things. In other words, the universe is intelligible, and he feels a deep sense of gratitude for this.

Some scientists embrace a philosophy that says everything can be reduced to atoms, but Polkinghorne disagrees. In *Beyond Science*, he argues that science cannot stand on such a simplistic foundation. The ..niverse has "become aware of itself". Conscious beings have emerged, and they – or rather, we – can even enjoy that awareness. For him, beauty and wonder are not imaginary constructs, but real experiences: signs that our world is "suffused with value". He believes that these values cannot be accounted for by the movement of atoms alone, because there are other levels of reality that are important besides the purely physical. Some physicists have searched for a "Grand Unified Theory", or "Theory of Everything", but Polkinghorne writes that "I actually believe that the grandest Unified Theory, the true Theory of Everything, is provided by belief in God".[189]

These three brief glimpses of scientist-theologians and their work show that a deeper knowledge of God leads to deeper wonder. Theology provides the tools to understand and interpret the experience of beauty and fascination in science, and take the conversation about science and religion forward into more interesting places than the usual debates and arguments.

God of wonders

For Rhoda Hawkins, the wonder she experiences in science has a very significant impact on her faith, and I found it easy to get her talking on this subject. She said, "When I experience wonder at the world around me – wonder at a particular system I've been studying – I have someone to attribute that to…" Because she believes God made the things she is studying, her response is different to that of some of her colleagues. "That wonder for me personally is also a wonder at God's creation. It's worship, in a sense."

Outside of work, Rhoda cultivates her sense of wonder by spending time in the countryside. She explained that "Wonder, in the sense of being amazed and impressed by God's creation around me, is important in my faith. Sometimes I can feel closer to God in the countryside, or on a mountainside, than I do in church. Being surrounded by nature makes me think of God."

Rhoda recently moved to Sheffield, and she is making the most of being so close to the Peak District. "I love the fact that I can just go from the city and see the countryside so quickly, and that's something I deliberately do at weekends or when I've got some time off. For me, it is a refilling of wonder…" The wonder she experiences in the hills is different to that of her scientific work, but "in some ways it's all connected, because it's all wonder at God's creation, be it at a microscopic level, or at the level of hills and valleys".

The intellectual wrestling – that very active kind of wonder – that Rhoda enjoys in science is also "absolutely crucial" for her faith. She enjoys being challenged about her thinking, and is always interested to talk to people who have other views. She described herself as "the sort of Christian who always has questions, who likes to think about things at a deeper level". There was a time when Rhoda was helping her younger sister with some school maths problems. Her sister said, "I don't understand why you like maths, it just makes my brain hurt!" Rhoda understood what she meant. "It makes my brain hurt too, but I love the challenge." She said that "in some ways, the doubts I have about what I believe are part of that as well. I enjoy grappling with them."

Rhoda often has questions about the way God acts in the world, but she sees that as a positive experience because it helps to keep her faith dynamic. "I really enjoy addressing those doubts, trying to think things through and talking to other people. The process is something that I enjoy because I come out at the end of a time of real questioning and doubts in a position where my faith is stronger." Grappling with questions at an intellectual level is also balanced by a more down-to-earth approach. Rhoda has experienced answers to prayer, so she keeps on praying and keeps thinking her questions through. "I carry on praying, holding in tension my own experiences of God with the mysteries that remain at an intellectual level."

One final story from Rhoda captured her sense of excitement at learning more about God. "I remember as a child being impressed by some of the older people in the church who were in their eighties. Some of these people had been Christians for decades, and as a young child that seemed such a long time! I thought, 'That's amazing, that they are still Christians and they still don't understand everything.' I found that really exciting: the idea that I could spend decades and decades learning more about God, and still not know it all, because it's like an adventure – an exploration where you're discovering more and more about God, in the way that science does. You don't know what's around the corner."

I appreciate Rhoda's honesty and the fact that she does not tidy all the loose ends of her faith out of sight. Her willingness to probe into difficult areas and unanswered questions is a challenge to anyone who says that faith is blind. I am also inspired by the fact that for her, this process is driven by a sense of wonder and adventure. Her picture of exploring a castle was particularly vivid – what's in the next room? Unlike François Jacob's analogy (in chapter two) of searching in dark rooms, Rhoda's journey of faith is one of wonder and fascination.

Wonder in the Bible

If wonder leads some scientists to God, does it tell us anything about him? Deane-Drummond thought not, but there at least are some questions to think about. First of all, does God wonder? We wonder, but if God is truly omniscient then surely he has nothing to wonder about? The Bible describes how God delights in the good things he sees in the world, but wonder always seems to be on the human side.

The French philosopher and Christian mystic Simone Weil pointed out that Genesis shows God's delight in appreciating others. God is three in one – so there could be that contemplation and wonder of others within God himself. Weil thinks that our ability to focus away from ourselves and enjoy other people is a reflection of God's sense of wonder.[190] Or perhaps, like imagination, we wonder simply because it is part of our commission: a gift so that we can fulfil our God-given potential on earth. Whatever its source, our ability to wonder seems to be a vital part of our humanness.

The Bible is full of awe and wonder, and the two concepts are closely linked. Hebrew scholars tell me that a number of different words are translated as "wonder": meaning something that is difficult to understand or beyond our capabilities to do, that is a sign from God. Biblical wonders caused amazement, but they also prompted people to ask questions about what God is like and what he was doing, and helped them pay attention to what was coming next. There are always more mentions of the word "wonder" than "awe" in any English translation of the Bible – in fact, about twice as many on average.[191] Perhaps this reflects something of the way God chooses to work. Thinking, curious, open-eyed wonder plays an important part in the life of faith.

The Old Testament is crammed full of accounts of God using "signs and wonders" to teach people what he is like. God does wonderful deeds (e.g. Exodus 15; Psalm 9), and his love and his Law are described as wonderful (e.g. Psalm 119). At this stage in history, people were building up a picture of what God is like. This culminates in the New Testament, and particularly the Gospels,[192] where God presents himself in human form. This is the ultimate revelation of God's character, and is quite unexpected. People had got into lazy ways of thinking, and lowered their sights so they were expecting less of God than he actually offered. Jesus challenged their preconceptions: their judgmentalism, legalism, and religiosity. People wondered at Jesus' miracles and teaching. They also wondered at the course of events. Why did God choose to come as a poor carpenter's son, and not a great statesman or warrior?

The story of Jesus' birth is especially marked by wonder: everyone involved in this extraordinary sequence of events is left wondering what is about to happen through this child. God doesn't always provide answers, but he does identify with us and make us think. Christianity definitely isn't about mindlessly following a set of rules – though that is often easier. As Olaf Pedersen quickly discovered in his physics lessons, a more roundabout and unexpected process can be a far more engaging and memorable teaching method.

In her book on wonder and wisdom, Celia Deane-Drummond pointed out that the most amazing and awe-inspiring events in the Bible are often ambiguous in their outcome. The Old Testament describes how people saw the most incredible miracles that convinced them God was taking care of them, but then they quickly forgot what God had done and returned to their old ways. This sequence of events happens over and over again, and especially in the book of Exodus. It's easy to forget the evidence for extraordinary things and fall back into more usual ways of thinking.

In the New Testament,[193] wonders provoked many people to think, and this resulted in a decision: either towards belief or disbelief. Unless people were listening to the whole of Jesus' teaching and open to what he had to say – in other words, developing wisdom – wonders alone wouldn't convince them that he was from God. Jesus knew this, so when people demanded a miraculous sign he never gave one (e.g. in Matthew 16). Unless wisdom is involved, developing deeper wonder, nothing happens.

Paying attention

So wonder is vitally important in both science and faith, and deeper understanding leads to deeper wonder. I will finish with an aspect of wonder that I have returned to time and time again in my own thinking, and it is the idea of cultivating wonder – this time in theology. I mentioned Jürgen Moltmann and Karl Barth in my chapter on beauty, and both of these men were passionate about the importance of wonder in their profession. Barth's insights about wonder at the person of God are vital for any Christian, and Moltmann's writing is relevant to everyone – whatever their beliefs might be.

Barth's book *Evangelical Theology* is about the human side of theology, and it contains a chapter on wonder that I found moving, challenging, and reassuring. I had been wondering how theologians manage to study God without losing perspective, but Barth was aware of that problem and he tackled it with great feeling. His words are very personal, and helped me to imagine him sitting in his study, lost in wonder.

According to Barth, wonder is important in theology because of the unique nature of the subject. How does a professional theologian actually go about their work? They are studying God, and if God is anything like what Christians say about him then studying him should be an eye-opening experience, to say the least. He wrote that "A quite specific astonishment stands at the beginning of every theological perception, inquiry, and thought, in fact at the root of every theological word. This astonishment is indispensable if theology is to exist..."

Barth was overwhelmed by the unique character of God's plan for saving us through the person of Jesus. He argued that if a Christian theologian isn't constantly amazed by God, they have missed the point and might as well give up:

> If anyone should *not* find himself astonished and
> filled with wonder when he becomes involved
> in one way or another with theology, he would
> be well advised to consider once more, from
> a certain remoteness and without prejudice,
> what is involved in this undertaking ... If such
> astonishment is lacking, the whole enterprise of
> even the best theologian would canker at the roots
> ... both he and theology would fare better if he
> would devote his time to some other occupation.

There is also the reassurance from Barth that

> as long as even a poor theologian is capable of
> astonishment, he is not lost to the fulfilment of
> his task. He remains serviceable as long as the
> possibility is left open that astonishment may seize
> him like an armed man.

Barth believed that a theologian should be humble and open to surprises: "... in theological wonder it is a sheer impossibility that he might one day finish his lessons, that the uncommon might become common, that the new might appear old and familiar, that the strange might ever become thoroughly domesticated." How else can one begin to approach a subject like the study of God, unless it is on one's knees – at least mentally if not literally?

For Barth, studying theology daily was a huge privilege. In his everyday work he was confronted with "the wondrous reality of the living *God*". He thought this should profoundly change the theologian in a way that was obvious to an outside observer, saying that "I become, am and remain something unknown, a different person, a stranger, when I am counted worthy to be permitted and required to wonder with respect to the wonder of God". These are the words of someone who has been profoundly touched by his exploration of theology.

Jürgen Moltmann's theological work has always centred around themes of hope, liberation for the poor and oppressed, and reconciliation. Wonder is an important part of the backdrop for his work and he has written[194] about the importance of cultivating an attitude of wonder. His work helped me to think about my own perceptions of the world, my relationships to others, and my attitude to God.

Like Chesterton, Moltmann thought we needed to pay more attention to what is going on around us. We must allow things to astonish us because only then will we see them properly. If we are open to new experiences, giving ourselves up to discovering what they have to show us, we learn. If we think we already know everything, we shut down our perceptions and stagnate.

According to Moltmann, the most astonishing thing we will encounter is the fact of our existence in the first place, and all our knowledge traces back to this first event. Wonder becomes lost in familiarity, but scientists, artists, and thinkers – and presumably also theologians – try to retain a childlike awareness and sense of wonder. It is important to remember the wonder of being, "Otherwise we could come to see only what we want to see, and go almost blindly through life."

Moltmann described how this type of wonder is also important in relationships. If people astonish us, we tend to pay attention and learn from them. "People whose unique character we respect continue to astonish us, and our wonder opens up the freedom for new future possibilities in our community with them." If we ceased to wonder, "we could cease to know other people because we have tethered ourselves fast to our pre-judgements about them, and simply want to have these confirmed."

In cultivating an attitude of wonderment, Moltmann writes, we are not simply sitting back and letting our minds absorb things passively. We are opening ourselves up to new avenues of intellectual exploration. Moltmann believed that humility is basic to our sense of wonder; it involves accepting that there is something greater than us or outside of our control, and that is also the best attitude to God. "Otherwise we could come to think that the products of our religious fantasy are God, and notice nothing of the living God."

Moltmann quotes the early theologian Gregory of Nyssa, saying that "Concepts are idols, only wonder understands…" In other words, if Christians try to theorize about God too much, we lose something. But if we can approach God in wonder we are open to what he is really like, as Moltmann describes.

The One we call God eludes our ideas, which nail him down, and our concepts, which try to bring him within our grasp; and yet he is closer to us than we ourselves … In "the darkness of the lived moment" we become aware of God's presence.

Conclusion: Science and wonders

So when we encounter beauty and complexity in the world we can respond in one of two ways. We might wonder about the mechanisms that produced such a sight and want to find out more. Wonder leads to science. Or we might start asking deep questions about the meaning of things: Why am I here? Do I have any significance in this vast place? Why is the world so beautiful and so terrible? In this way, wonder also leads to theology. While these two responses are different, people like Rhoda have shown that they are not mutually exclusive.

In any sort of exploration, scientific or theological, there's a delicate balance to be found between scepticism and credulity. Wisdom must direct the process of enquiry and prevent self-deception. Richard Dawkins has said about science that

it goes on and on uncovering things. This doesn't mean we should believe just anything that anybody might dream up: there are a million things we can imagine but which are highly unlikely to be real – fairies and hobgoblins, leprechauns and hippogriffs. We should always be open minded, but the only good reason to believe

that something exists is if there is real evidence
that it does.[195]

I believe that Dawkins' principle applies to the whole of life, although I think evidence should include areas outside of science: art, the humanities, philosophy, theology, human experience, and relationships. Despite our best efforts we could make a mistake and fool ourselves, but we have to live within some sort of framework, so we might as well explore which is the best match to reality. If knowledge begins in wonder, we won't be satisfied with pat answers.

If knowledge also continues in wonder, then scientists like Rhoda can enjoy their work more fully, and theology will be as exciting as Barth meant it to be. Alister McGrath said that theology

> means being confronted with something so great
> that we cannot fully comprehend it, and so must
> do the best that we can with the analytical and
> descriptive tools at our disposal. Come to think
> of it, that is what the natural sciences aim to do as
> well.[196]

In the end, wonder is an antidote to excessive scepticism. It's easy to slip into thinking that science has ruled out wonders, but if God is who he says he is, that is just what I expect of him. This act of wonder is not gullibility, but a "humble openness to possibility".[197] As any scientist knows, "Reality is always more surprising than we are capable of imagining."[198]

Chapter 8

Awe

I once had a moment of awe in an exam. I had just written a long essay explaining how DNA is copied from cell to cell,[200] and was relieved that I had managed to remember all the different steps involved. At the end, I wrote about the accuracy of this replication. If I were to retype all of the 45,000 or so letters and spaces that make up this chapter I would probably make a few mistakes, even after spell-checking. But only one mistake is left uncorrected for every ten thousand million A, T, C or G subunits that are added to the DNA chain.[201] That's an astonishing figure, and I stopped for a minute to think about it.

DNA replication is not just accurate, it's also fast. When one of our own cells replicates its DNA, it adds about 670,000 subunits every minute.[202] I had not given this much thought until I sat in the exam with a few minutes to spare. I was staggered that such tiny and seemingly fragile machinery could act so quickly and with such precision. I waxed lyrical about all this for a few sentences at the end of my essay, but I never found out whether my musings earned me any extra marks.

Another sub-microscopic event that I learned about at university was the generation of energy in our bodies. All the carbohydrates, fats, and proteins we eat are digested and broken down in a series of chemical reactions to produce large quantities of a simple molecule called acetate.[203] Acetate is then combined with oxygen in a series of chemical reactions that generate enough energy-rich molecules to power every activity of our bodies.

This process is called the Krebs cycle,[204] and what fills me with awe is its intricacy. There is incredible detail here: a chain reaction of molecules that would look very uninteresting in a test tube but are vital for keeping us alive. The cycle is robust: these reactions will continue to happen inside our bodies whether we look after them or not. And on a global scale, it is incredibly powerful. The Krebs cycle was happening long before words of any kind – let alone "Krebs" – were articulated by human beings, and it occurs in every oxygen-using organism[205] on the planet. Our best efforts to replicate this system would, I expect, result in a clumsy copy that lacked the compactness and precision of the original pathway in a living organism.

I don't expect everyone to share my feelings about biochemical reactions, but if you spend time looking at the stars, reading about the latest discoveries, or watching a good science documentary, you might find yourself feeling in a similar state of stunned amazement.

Most scientists will have this sort of emotional response to their work from time to time. These are the high points: a reward for long days in the lab, or demanding field trips. Finally something is understood, and it stops you in your tracks. Or maybe you see something unexpectedly beautiful and intricate. There might be an element of fear as well as delight, admiration or respect, even reverence, as you take it in. As with wonder, greater understanding can deepen our sense of awe, so there is a rational as well as an emotional element involved in these feelings.

At times during the writing of this book I have felt like the writer of a medical drama who collects the most dramatic moments in a person's career and packs them all into a single episode. I have chosen the highlights, but in between are days, weeks, or months of hard slog and regular disappointments. If wonder is fairly common, full-blown awe only comes at rare moments. These are often the most memorable moments in a scientist's career. You call others over to look, or spend time explaining what happened. You tell and retell the story in different ways. Most importantly, awe can prompt a whole range of responses: scientific, aesthetic, philosophical, ethical, and perhaps even spiritual.

This chapter is the culmination of my exploration of how science enhances faith, and also the most God-centred. Creativity and imagination play a vital part in both science and the life of faith. Beauty and wonder may be almost daily experiences, depending on the field of research, and invite us to think about why we appreciate those moments.

Awe, on the other hand, is less common and almost always accompanied by spiritual-sounding language. For Christians, there is a strong link between awe and worship of God, so I will explore that connection in the last part of the chapter, looking at how science itself can be a form of worship.

Awesome predators

To find out more about awe in science I met with Bob Sluka, a marine conservationist from the US who currently works in Oxfordshire and Kenya. So far all the scientists I had interviewed were lab-based, but Bob works in the field – or rather, the sea. I felt that it was important to include someone whose work takes them outdoors and into more direct contact with nature, and who also works at a larger scale than some of the other scientists featured. Bob is unusual because his faith is not just part of the background of his work – it is included in his job description. In his work with *A Rocha*, a Christian conservation organization, he draws on both scientific research and Christian theology to build conservation programmes that have a lasting impact on whole communities.

Bob's route into marine biology started with a love of scuba diving. He enjoyed science, so when he found out that he could get a degree that involved diving, he grabbed the opportunity with both hands. After ten years of study and research training, he became a coral reef fish ecologist. A large part of the reason why Bob chose to work in the sea, and why he still enjoys it now, is the sense of awe and wonder that he feels when he sees rare or especially beautiful things.

Bob told me about one experience in particular that

convinced him he wanted to be a marine biologist. "During my studies, I did a lot of scuba diving in the Bahamas. One of the areas we studied was a marine reserve in a beautiful little island chain called the Exuma Cays. Part of my research was to find out whether this marine park was doing what it was supposed to be doing. In other words, was there any difference between the numbers of fish inside versus outside of the park?

"In Exuma Cays the water is quite shallow, and crystal clear, so we could almost count the fish from the top of the boat. But one day our job was to go out into deeper water and count the fish there. We swam through the reef to the edge where it drops straight down into a 2,000-metre trench called 'the tongue of the ocean'. Swimming off the reef felt like going over the edge of a cliff, but we stayed there, hanging out in open water looking at the cliff wall and trying to count fish.

"When you're in deep water, it's dark. So you're looking over your shoulder every once in a while, and then you glance down and get that feeling... One time I looked down and there was a shape moving way below. I couldn't really see what it was, so I kept an eye on it. I looked down again and noticed it was getting bigger and bigger. Suddenly something swam past me with the force of a jet. I looked up and right there was a huge barracuda, staring at me with its big eyes and big teeth.

"At first I was afraid because my dive buddy was a long way away, but then my training kicked in and I remembered that these fish don't normally bite. My fear turned into awe, and I was able to enjoy sitting out in the ocean looking eye to eye with this beautiful creature. I thought, 'This is something that I want to protect. This is something I enjoy, and it's worth spending my time caring for it.'"

Humility

Experiences like Bob's are not isolated. Many of his colleagues and former classmates are driven by the same motivations. One friend studies frogs, and regularly posts amazing photographs of them on the internet. Another works with alligators, and his enthusiasm has earned him his own show on the National Geographic channel. For all of these people, awe is an experience to be enjoyed and cultivated.

What is it that makes us feel awe at times, rather than just wonder? When scientists use the word "awe", they are usually thinking of things that are unexpectedly intricate, precise, ordered, powerful in some way, and perhaps also beautiful. There's a sense of being bowled over, or arrested. If wondering is an active experience, then awe is more about standing still and appreciating or being inspired by something. Awe often involves a sense of vastness because of the scale, number, or complexity of what is seen.[206] Although the knowledge is there, it's difficult to hold it together.

Feeling overwhelmed is usually a negative experience when you are trying to complete a task or manage something physically, but it can be very positive in an intellectual context. For example, it is almost impossible to grasp the scale of the universe, but feeling a sense of awe at its size can be very inspiring – and then wonder takes over. If you're a certain sort of person, after a few minutes gazing at the stars and feeling small you might set about finding out some numbers or trying to imagine a scale model.

If the sun is the size of a small melon, earth is a peppercorn sitting twenty-six paces away. Mars is a pinhead another fourteen paces away, and Jupiter a chestnut ninety-five paces from Mars. Pluto is a grain of sand almost a kilometre from the sun, and the cloud of space-dust that marks the limit of our solar system is 3,200 miles away. The nearest star, Proxima Centauri, is another 3,200 miles beyond that. So if your sun-melon is in London, the next closest star is in Chicago. If you then multiply your pace by 3,600, that gives the actual scale of the universe.[207]

I heard the astronomer Jocelyn Bell Burnell speak in Cambridge recently, and someone in the audience asked her how she held these huge scales in her head. Her answer was that she didn't. You have to forget the actual size of things most of the time and just work with mathematical shorthand, or you couldn't function properly. She clearly enjoys the times when she explains the numbers to people, and both she and the audience can enjoy a sense of awe, but most of the time that feeling is lost in the day-to-day routine. So as well as being a more powerful feeling than wonder, awe is also more rare – or at least harder to sustain.

Awe-inspiring experiences can also include an element of incomprehensibility. A scientist's work can sometimes feel limitless. How much more is there to find out? Recognizing that what is known is just the tip of the iceberg can bring a sense of smallness and humility. Isaac Newton may have felt this when he wrote:

I do not know what I may appear to the world;
but to myself I seem to have been only like a boy,
playing on the sea shore, and diverting myself,
in now and then finding a smoother pebble or a

prettier shell than ordinary, whilst the great ocean
of truth lay all undiscovered before me.[208]

Galileo expressed a similar thought in his book about the
solar system. He wrote that "anyone who has experienced
just once the perfect understanding of one single thing,
and has truly tasted what knowledge consists of, would
recognise that of the infinity of other truths he understands
nothing".[209] I find that the more senior a scientist is, the
more likely they are to have realized this, and to express
amazement that they are able to even find anything out at
all.

Mountains

During my exploration of this topic, I noticed that when
scientists are describing the process of discovery, they often
use the analogy of climbing a mountain. Being interested in
mountains myself, I began to gather these stories together. I have
already shared Rhoda Hawkins' account of wonder pushing her
to "climb the mountain", but most of the others in my collection
are about reaching the top and feeling a sense of awe.

A new scientific theory provides a vantage point from
which to make sense of all the data, so it can feel as if you are
looking down from a great height on a whole panorama of
information, some familiar and some unfamiliar. Suddenly
the data you have been wrestling with make sense, and
everything comes clear. You might feel small in the face of a
vast and largely unexplored landscape. You are gripped by a
powerful sense of awe, and the elation of achievement.

Heisenberg captured this experience particularly well when he wrote about his work on atomic theory:

> The last few weeks have been very exciting for me. Perhaps an analogy is the best way of describing my experiment: that of the attempt to attain the summit of atomic theory which is still unknown, an attempt which has required great efforts of me over the last five years. And now the summit is there in front of me; the whole area of internal relations in atomic theory is unexpectedly and clearly spread out before my eyes. What these internal relations show in all their mathematic abstraction, an incredible degree of simplicity, is a gift that we can only accept with humility.[210]

For the molecular biologist Max Perutz this feeling was a natural high:

> A discovery is like falling in love and reaching the top of a mountain after a hard climb all in one, an ecstasy not induced by drugs but by the revelation of a face of nature that no one has seen before and that often turns out to be more subtle and wonderful than anyone had imagined.[211] In these mountaintop moments, finally the mist clears, and the scientist can see a long way intellectually. You can rest and feel restored after the hard slog. Enrique Mota, a mathematician at the University of Valencia, said that reaching the solution to

a difficult problem is like reaching the top of a mountain. The sun comes out, you enjoy the view down the valley and you feel refreshed. In describing the problem and showing the solution, you feel at ease because a sense of order has been restored.[212]

Intellectual mountaineering was a way of life for Einstein: a calm contemplation of the order of things that was closer to meditation than conquering:

A finely tempered nature longs to escape from personal life into the world of objective perception and thought; this desire may be compared with the townsman's irresistible longing to escape from his noisy, cramped surroundings into the silence of high mountains, where the eye ranges freely through the still, pure air and fondly traces out the restful contours apparently built for eternity.[213]

Jeff Hardin described the difference that being a Christian made to his experience of awe, quoting a well-known theoretical chemist: "Fritz Schaefer was mentioned a number of years ago in an American news magazine as saying, 'The significance and joy in my science comes in the occasional moments of discovering something new and saying to myself, "So that's how God did it!"'"[214] For Jeff, "The moment is like when you go on a hike and there's a special spot at the end, on top of a promontory with a beautiful view that not very many people know about. When you get to it for the first time and see that wonderful vista, for most people the natural response is to want to share it with somebody, and I think the same is true in science. As a Christian I want to share that discovery with God himself."

Ocean

As I have already described, working in the open sea means that some of Bob's experiences of awe involve a large dose of fear. On another occasion he was surrounded in shallow water by a shoal of "small" (metre-long) barracuda. They circled around him as if he was their prey, and only his knowledge that they would not be able to get their mouths around him kept him from panicking. He was able to calm his fears and enjoy another moment of awe, watching the sunset and this great school of fish.

Understanding what you're seeing can also increase that sense of awe. Bob described how he and his son saw a mantis shrimp, a common but shy lobster-like creature, in a rock pool in Kenya. They caught sight of a flash of brilliant colour, and were able to observe it for just a few fleeting moments as it fled back to its burrow. Often these rare glimpses are remembered most intensely. "It's like, there it is! And it's gone," said Bob, "and it just takes your breath away."

The sighting of a mantis shrimp was a shared experience of awe, and that is often the way for Bob. For him, awe can be a feeling that comes on reflection, when he's back on dry land and telling others about what he saw. Seeing other people's reactions – like his son's strong memories of the mantis shrimp (he made a model of it in an art class when they got home) – helps Bob to recognize the value of what he has seen. He often takes his family on field trips, and said, "With kids you see things through their eyes. They pick up an insect that you've walked over millions of times, and you start looking at it afresh, and that does help increase your appreciation for it."

Transcendence

So where do these feelings of awe lead? For some, there is a sense of a mystery to be solved. Richard Feynman, a theoretical physicist who worked on the way that light and matter interact (known as quantum electrodynamics), wrote that

> The same thrill, the same awe and mystery, come again and again when we look at any problem deeply enough. With more knowledge comes deeper, more wonderful mystery, luring one on to penetrate deeper still. Never concerned that the answer may prove disappointing, but with pleasure and confidence we turn over each new stone to find unimagined strangeness leading on to more wonderful questions and mysteries – certainly a grand adventure![215]

For others, awe leads them beyond science. The theologian and philosopher Austin Farrar wrote that a scientist may experience

> constant amazement at the ... world which yields such complex and ordered responses to

his yardstick method. But this amazement,
this almost religious awe, does not find direct
expression in his scientific activity; in so far
as he entertains such feelings, he is more of a
metaphysician than a pure scientist. That is only
another way of saying, that as well as being a
scientist he is a man: and indeed, most scientists
are human.[216]

When Einstein used the word mystery, he meant something more spiritual. In what he called *My Credo*, Einstein wrote, "The most beautiful and deepest experience a man can have is the sense of the mysterious. It is the underlying principle of religion as well as of all serious endeavour in art and science." For him, there was a "sense that behind anything that can be experienced there is something that our minds cannot grasp, whose beauty and sublimity reaches us only indirectly".[217]

For the Jesuit philosopher Enrico Cantore, this contact with something beyond science was a form of knowledge. After interviewing a number of scientists, he came to the conclusion that the mystery of the universe lies not in ignorance, but in something *so* intelligible that we sometimes cannot take it in. Being overwhelmed by a sense of something greater beyond science feels not like the darkness of unknowing, but "like the darkness that is felt when one is overwhelmed by dazzling light".[218]

These are glimpses of what Alister McGrath would call "the transcendent": experiences – whether in science or another area of life – that reach beyond the realm of normal human experience. But what is actually happening at these times? What is going on in the mind of the researcher? McGrath described three ways in which this can happen.[219]

First, there might be a flash of unexpected clarity or epiphany, when suddenly things make sense. This is a very significant and privileged insight, completely detached from their normal view of the world. These moments are usually fleeting, and can't be scheduled – they just happen. The person is changed by their experience, and might feel a sense of anti-climax afterwards.

Another way of encountering the transcendent is when someone is struck by a deep truth about the "unity of reality". This could be described as a mystical experience, because it is difficult to explain. Again, it is a short, unpredictable moment which has a significant impact on the person involved. Finally, someone might feel what the theologian Rudolf Otto called a sense of the "numinous". There is something there, something "wholly other", that the person involved is in contact with, but which cannot be accounted for by any physical explanation.

It is difficult to find examples for these experiences because they are very personal, and by definition they are difficult to describe, but I can make a couple of guesses. One comes from my time as a PhD student. I was working in the fish room, sitting next to someone from another research group, and we were both examining zebrafish larvae. As we stared down our microscopes we talked about how much we enjoyed working with zebrafish and watching them grow. My colleague told me that he occasionally had a moment when he realized how incredible nature is, and felt what sounded to me like a deep sense of awe – although I can't remember him using that word. For him, those rare experiences were one of the reasons why he wanted to stay in research and become a lecturer. He wanted to share his experience with others and help them to appreciate nature in the same way.

Another example comes from Edwin Hubble, the astronomer who found that the universe is expanding. He may have been describing a sense of the numinous when he wrote the following:

> … sometimes, through a strong, compelling experience of mystical insight, a man knows beyond the shadow of doubt that he has been in touch with a reality that lies behind mere phenomena. He himself is completely convinced, but he cannot communicate the certainty. It is a private revelation. He may be right, but unless we share his ecstasy we cannot know.[220]

Whether or not any of these people have experienced anything transcendent, it is clear that they have been changed by their work. They have experienced a powerful sense of awe, and that is one of the driving forces or rewards for their work in the lab or field.

God

Einstein used the word "God" in his more popular writing. This God is sometimes interpreted to be the personal God of Judaism, but that isn't what was meant. Einstein wrote that "a belief bound up with deep feeling, in a superior mind that reveals itself in the world of experience, represents my conception of God".[221] So his religion was simply to explore the work of this Mind in nature, to "wonder at these secrets and to attempt humbly to grasp with my mind a mere image of the lofty structure of all there is".[222]

For other scientists, God *is* personal, and their awe enhances their faith. Shannon Stahl, a Professor of Chemistry from the University of Madison-Wisconsin, described to me an experience of the transcendent that he occasionally has in his work. He said that whenever he writes a major grant proposal, he experiences a burst of creativity and inspiration. "It's as if I see the world differently. I see how the ideas fit together in a way that I never did before, and I think, 'Oh it's so obvious', because all of a sudden it just makes sense. I don't deal with equations so much but it's as if, all of a sudden, I have an equation that describes everything."

At those times, Stahl said, "It's like being 'at one with the universe'. Recently I realized that the Jews call this 'shalom', where everything is at peace and in harmony … I think there is something so beautiful about science when it fits and you get that inspiration. It's otherworldly." Stahl is a Christian, and to him this is a spiritual experience. "Clearly something that is bigger than myself has all of a sudden taken hold of me and lifted me up."[223]

Bob Sluka also has this sense of peacefulness in his work. When his fear at a potentially risky situation diminishes and he can begin to enjoy an encounter with nature, he feels a sense of peace and God's presence. At these times, Bob is aware that he is part of a much bigger picture. "A lot of marine life remains hidden, so you're seeing things that God delights in but they don't really have any reference to or utility to us. There are rock pools on the coast in Kenya that are exposed just for an hour or two at low tide and then covered up, and if you go out there at the wrong time you just see water. You think there's nothing there, and then the tide goes out and reveals something that, for the most part, only God gets to look at. So for me the spiritual side of awe can be a peacefulness and resting in being part of something that God has made."

Strength, harnessed

Like Bob, I have found that science gives me a sense of awe which enlarges my view of God. We live in an incomprehensibly large and beautiful universe, on a planet containing a huge diversity of intricately structured organisms. God must be incomparably powerful and intelligent, patient, generous, and creative.

Jocelyn Bell Burnell found it hard to maintain her sense of awe at the scale of the universe, and I often struggle to maintain my own sense of awe at God. In fact, as Bell Burnell said, if I could it would be hard to function normally. The Roman Catholic theologian Jame Schaefer said that "Our entrenchment in a part of [the universe] and our condition as mortal beings prevent us from intellectually grasping the universe in its entirety",[224] and something similar applies to our view of God. Our minds are too small to take him in completely. This is like Cantore's "dazzling intelligibility" of the world, but applied instead to God.

An unexpected example of how science can expand our view of God came to me as I finished reading Richard

Dawkins' book *The God Delusion*. In the last section of the book, "The mother of all burkas", there is a wonderful description of how science opens our eyes to the world. If you can ignore the negative rhetoric (you could think of looking through an opening in a tent) and focus on the science, this piece of writing can be a powerful call to worship the God who made everything that science reveals to us:

> Our eyes see the world through a narrow slit in the electromagnetic spectrum. Visible light is a chink of brightness in the vast dark spectrum, from radio waves at the long end to gamma rays at the short end. Quite how narrow is hard to appreciate and a challenge to convey. Imagine a gigantic black burka, with a vision slit of approximately the standard width, say about one inch ... The one-inch window of visible light is derisorily tiny compared with the miles and miles of black cloth representing the invisible part of the spectrum, from radio waves at the hem of the skirt to gamma rays at the top of the head. What science does for us is widen the window. It opens up so wide that the imprisoning black garment drops away almost completely, exposing our senses to airy and exhilarating freedom.

Dawkins then goes on to show how science opens a window on a world more fantastic than we could ever have imagined. The petals of flowers are dotted with patches that reflect UV light, creating spots and stripes that only insects can see. Telescopes detect X-rays and radio waves from distant objects in space. Infrared radiation is emitted by warm bodies, and radio waves can be harnessed to transmit music. This is the world I believe God made.

After reading Dawkins, I immediately turned to Luke chapter 8, which describes Jesus bringing a dead girl back to life. With my imagination still in the invisible world revealed by science, I saw Jesus as the one who knows the universe inside out and – more importantly – spoke it into being.[225] How did Jesus raise people from the dead? Obviously we won't be able to understand how that works in scientific terms, but I'm not surprised that God can work outside of the usual laws of physics from time to time.

In the Bible there is no separate word for awe. The Hebrew word *yārē'*, I am told, essentially means "fear", but is translated as either fear or awe, depending on the context. But the God of the Bible is not just to be feared. The healing described in Luke and others like it show me that yes, God is the awe-inspiring creator of the universe, but he also uses his power in incredibly gentle ways.

I discovered a good way to describe this tension between the awesomeness and intimacy of God during a weekend at the Lee Abbey retreat centre in Devon. John Bryant[226] was the speaker, and he used the first chapter of John and the description of God's creative power in Job chapter 38 as a basis for a reflection on the relationship between science and faith. The Warden of Lee Abbey, Revd David Rowe, then took this theme forward in his sermon on Sunday, using the same

Bible passages. At one point he asked the question, "How does God manage to communicate with us without turning us into dust and ashes?"

To answer his own question, David used the painting *Christ Before the High Priest* by the seventeenth-century Dutch painter Gerrit van Honthorst. This picture shows Jesus standing in front of a table, brightly illuminated by the light of a single candle. He is dishevelled from his arrest, but authoritative, and he has his head on one side as if to concentrate on what is being said to him. The High Priest, on the other hand, sits behind the table in the shadows, his finger pointing accusingly at Jesus. The soldiers who made the arrest are barely visible, huddled in a corner. There is a huge contrast between the assumed authority of the priest, and Jesus' real authority as he stands over him, dignified and restrained.

Rowe said that we don't use the word "meekness" very often, but its original meaning was something like "strength, harnessed". Jesus could have blasted the High Priest and everyone else to smithereens, but he didn't even waste time arguing. He knew he was there to display his love for everyone, including the man confronting him. This is not the God that science reveals, but how God chooses to reveal himself. Real power can be used in gentle as well as spectacular ways.

Paradox

Bob Sluka's own faith journey demonstrates much of what I have been saying about awe in both science and Christianity. He came from a fairly conservative American evangelical background, and at first science seemed to have no relevance to his faith. After graduating he was offered a job helping to set up a marine biology lab in the Maldives, and Bob saw this as an opportunity to do what he enjoyed, as well as getting involved in what he thought was more important work in building relationships with local communities. He and his family spent ten years in South Asia – first in the Maldives and then in India – studying coral reefs, and also working in a holistic way with the people in those countries.

It was only when Bob moved to England, where he consults for the Christian conservation group *A Rocha*, that he began to see how his faith and his scientific activities could complement each other. He said that "A major turning point was becoming involved with Christians in Science and going to their annual conference, where I finally realized that marine conservation is an expression of my faith, and is service to God in and of itself".

Bob explained that one of the good things about American evangelicalism is an emphasis on a personal relationship with Jesus. "My dad introduced me to the work of Francis Schaeffer, the theologian and philosopher who set up the L'Abri Fellowship. In his book *Pollution and the Death of Man*, Schaeffer writes about the infinite and the personal aspects of the character of God." Most of Bob's Christian life had been focused on developing his personal relationship with Christ, but that changed when he moved to England. "In embracing all of the truth of science, and also exploring the infinity of God and what the theologian Richard Bauckham would call the community of creation, I have realized that I do have a special relationship with God, but I am also a creature: I am something that's created."

He said, "It's hard to hold the infinite and the personal natures of God in tension. To me, one of the greatest evidences of the reality of Christianity are the paradoxes in it ... It's not black and white this way, or black and white that way, but you have to somehow balance those two things. I'm just a creature – like the man Job in the Bible I'm someone who needs to be put in his place all the time by the creation around me – and yet I'm a child of God who can speak directly to the Father.

"Science has helped me to understand my place in creation, and that has made me realize just how amazing Jesus' death on the cross was. If the cross was all about rescuing humans from death, then it's all about me and I could almost feel as if I deserve it. But in the context of the vastness of time and space, I find it easier to understand the reality that God didn't have to send Jesus. Science has helped me to realize how special Jesus' death and resurrection really is, and also how comprehensive it is. Theologians talk about four events: creation, fall (human wrongdoing and its consequences), redemption (because of what Jesus did), and new creation (the renewal of the world at the end of time). Christians often like to focus on the fall and redemption, but it's important to put those two events in the context of creation and new creation. If *everything* broke at the fall, then Jesus' death on the cross is not just for us – it is for all of creation. It's about God, and not primarily about me.

"Now I can hardly talk about science without theology, and about theology without science. Understanding who I am as a creation of God is helping me to value my relationship with him even more, and part of my work is to help Christians understand that.[227] The more I look into science, the more I'm awed by God."

Worshipping God in science

For most Christians working in science, their work helps them to worship. The dazzling intelligibility of the world increases our humility before an awesome God, and worship happens for a scientist when they turn that humility and awe towards God and thank him for the universe he has made. As Jeff Hardin said when he talked about his mountaintop moments of discovery, sharing that experience with God "turns the process of discovery into an act of worship".

So scientific research itself can be done as an act of worship. Christians are encouraged to offer their work to God, and there is a long tradition of scientists doing this. I have already mentioned the sixteenth-century astronomer Johannes Kepler and his scientific vocation.[228] He saw his work as an act of worship, and his scientific writing was interspersed with prayers and hymns.

One of the most famous of Kepler's prayers comes at the end of his most famous book, *The Harmony of the World*, which lays out his third law of planetary motion, and it is a beautiful dedication of his work to God:

> If I have been enticed into rashness by the
> wonderful beauty of thy works, or if I have loved
> my own glory among men, while advancing in
> work destined for thy glory, gently and mercifully
> pardon me; and finally, deign graciously to cause

that these demonstrations may lead to thy glory
and to the salvation of souls, and nowhere be an
obstacle to that. Amen.

I have also written about the seventeenth-century botanist
Revd Dr John Ray, and there is a wonderful story of him
when he was lecturing at Trinity College, Cambridge.[229] Ray
regularly preached in the college chapel, and botany was such
an important part of his worship that he also held some of his
lectures in there. I can't imagine that happening today, but
I wonder what effect it would have on the students if they
learned in such surroundings?

In *Beauty*, Jeff Hardin also mentioned that the composer
Johann Sebastian Bach adopted the Jesuit tradition of writing
J. J., short for *Jesu juva* (Jesus help me), at the beginning of
every piece of work, and S. D. G., short for *Soli Deo Gloria*
(glory to God alone), at the end. Catherine Crouch, a physics
professor from Swarthmore College, was inspired to do the
same in her laboratory notebooks and lecture notes: a tangible
reminder of God's hand in everything she does.[230]

Another scientist wrote *Soli Deo Gloria* in the dedication
at the end of his PhD thesis. I met Fernando Caballero, a
paleontologist who works on microscopic marine plankton
fossils, at the annual conference of the Spanish Christians in
Science group. He told me about what he had written, and
what happened next. "After my thesis examination we had
an informal lunch with the examiners, and the conversation
centred around this quote. All the people there were asking
me, 'What do you think?' or 'What do you believe?'

"Later on, one of the other examiners wrote to me. At

first I was afraid that he was upset with me, but he said, 'To your "*Soli Deo Gloria*", I say "Magnus in magnis, maximus in minimis"', which is a quote attributed to Augustine: 'God is great in the big things, but is greatest in the small things.' I was very surprised that he should encourage me in this way, because he was not a religious man. It was strange that this person who I admired scientifically thought the same as me: that these small fossils are so great, and reveal something about God."[231] Like Fernando, virtually every Christian that I speak to in science is acutely aware that their work is an expression of their worship to God, and looks for similar ways to express that either privately or publicly.

Another form of worship comes from the results of science. Sooner or later, scientific knowledge is used to develop new technologies. How those technologies are developed and used is also part of a Christian's worship of God. Chapter 21 of Revelation describes how the "kings of the earth will bring their splendour" into the city of God. Will that splendour include the best of our scientific and technological output, beautiful writing, and fine craftsmanship? It's both humbling and inspiring to think that work done now as an act of worship might last into eternity.[232]

Worshipping God with science

Enjoyment of creation at some level has often played a part in fostering worship for all Christians – not just scientists – and there are ways in which modern science can feed into that. Monasteries often include open spaces or gardens where people can draw near to God through being surrounded by nature; ancient manuscripts were embellished with pictures of animals and plants, and traditional church buildings and cathedrals usually contain some natural motifs.

An extraordinary example of science in church architecture can be found in St Mary's Church at Wreay, in Cumbria. It was here that Sarah Losh, a Victorian landowner, applied her great wealth and academic talents to create a building that reflected the full beauty and variety of life on earth. Inspired by naturalists and fossil hunters, Losh commissioned a huge number of carvings of animals and plants in stone and wood. Some of the windows are covered with translucent alabaster with fossil designs, and even some of the church furniture comes in the shape of animals or trees. The result is an inspiring riot of form and colour that might be a bit distracting for worshippers, but certainly displays the latest findings of science at the time.[233]

A more recent example of science in church architecture comes from St Crispin's Church in Leicester. This congregation recently commissioned a large and very beautiful window that uses scientific images to illustrate God's creation of humankind. Adam and Eve reach out from within a matrix of nerve cells, surrounded by a circular border of chromosomes and stars. Beyond the border, the hands of God stretch down to create different kinds of animals and plants. Perhaps other churches could move from the traditional bunch of flowers at the front to a more exuberant worship of God the creator in their buildings?

And what about sung worship? The Psalms are very early examples of worship songs that express joy at the wonder of creation. In other parts of the Bible the immensity and grandeur of nature is also used to invoke a feeling of awe and worship. Perhaps the most powerful expression of this is found in the book of Job, where God describes the great sweep of his creative work (chapters 38–41). We now understand some parts of the processes described – including the formation of the earth, weather, and animal behaviour – but the whole universe is just as awesome as it was thousands of years ago, and just as challenging to human understanding. As Job says in chapter 26, "And these are but the outer fringe of his works; how faint the whisper we hear of him! Who then can understand the thunder of his power?"

The writers of the Psalms wrote about stars using the most up-to-date knowledge of their day. Cutting-edge astronomers in the first millennium BC knew that the stars had come into existence at some point – they were created (e.g. Psalm 8); they had their names and places (e.g. Psalm 147); and they (on the whole) kept to those places and danced their set dances every year (e.g. Psalm 136).

There is now a wealth of contemporary hymns and songs that echo the psalmist's theme, but while science has moved on, the language of the songs often remains rooted in that ancient form of science. Some of the newer worship writers make references to galaxies or burning stars, and that's about as far as it goes. I'm not suggesting that we get rid of the old hymns, use lyrics that might be divisive in a church context, or tie ourselves in knots with technical jargon (I don't think I could sing about DNA transcription with a straight face!), but wouldn't it be good to praise God for some of the things that have been discovered in the last few hundred years?

I was at a meeting some time ago, where someone prayed to thank God for his efficiency in nature. Efficiency? Free energy from the sun, wind, and waves? Plants that produce food from sunshine, air, and water? The earth's crust packed full of useful ores and precious stones? These are examples of God's great generosity in producing an abundance of natural resources. Science helps me to praise God for his immense provision. Of course we need to think about how these resources can be used sustainably and distributed fairly, but they are provided on a spectacular scale. Could church harvest celebrations include thanks to God for *all* natural products?

Another source of fuel for worship comes from space. The unmanned voyager telescopes have been sent billions of kilometres from earth, reaching beyond the solar system,[234] and images from the Hubble telescope grace our computer monitors and television screens every day. Before high-resolution data was available astronomers could only guess at some of the details, but now a clearer picture has emerged – quite literally. These photographs have made their way into devotional books, but could they also inspire new hymns?

The senior project scientist for the Hubble Space Telescope is Dr Jennifer Wiseman, a Christian who is very involved in the science-faith dialogue, and also in research into planetary formation. Wiseman has said that

> Our worship of the Risen Christ should …
> acknowledge not only His victory over sin and
> death but also His Lordship over all time and
> space. In this way, scientific discovery can lift the
> minds and hearts of believers to a deeper level of

awe and reverence for the King of Kings and Lord
of Lords who is also Lord of all creation.[235]

The Christian songwriter and astronomy enthusiast Matt
Redman has written that Christians sometimes manage
to "take the extraordinary revelation of God and somehow
manage to make Him sound completely ordinary". Science
has the power to expand our horizons and shows how great
God is. As Redman said, "The highest mountain peaks
and the deepest canyon depths are just tiny echoes of His
proclaimed greatness. And the brightest stars above, only the
faintest emblems of the full measure of His glory."[236]

Bob Sluka is actively involved in helping Christians
worship God with his own work in marine biology.
"Historically, the wilderness was a place where people went
to seek God, and they put themselves in a place where it was
hard to survive, but they were also experiencing something
new and could listen to God ... Since I moved from seeing
my science not as a hobby or a means to other Christian
ends (i.e. serving people or reducing poverty), but as worship
itself and important to God, I have tried to cultivate a habit
of translating the beauty, wonder and awe that I experience
in that great wilderness, the ocean, into worship of God at
various levels.

"Part of my role as a researcher is to take what's hidden
from most people's sight under the water and let people see
this amazing thing that God has done. I also like to read,
so part of how I worship God is through writing an article
that captures those experiences and interprets them through
the lens of a biblical framework. For me, the writing process

is a way of giving glory to God and worshipping him, and sharing that with other people."

Finally, a Christian can worship God through taking care of creation. In his book *Song of a Scientist*, the environmental scientist Calvin DeWitt describes how Christians sing from two books: the book of God's creation and the book of his revelation, the Bible. In the past, people had a strong sense of being God's creatures, alongside the other creatures he had created, and all creation praises God together. Psalm 148 is a vivid description of this: "Praise the Lord from the earth … you mountains and all hills … wild animals and all cattle … young men and women, old men and children." More recently, writes DeWitt, Christians have lost sight of their creatureliness, and a dimension of worship along with it. Our relationship with the rest of creation has been broken, leading to climate change, destruction of habitats, and a loss of species at an alarming rate.

Like Sluka, DeWitt also appreciates the work of Richard Bauckham, who has written that "The best way to learn to value other creatures is to learn to worship with them." Other creatures praise God by being themselves, and by preserving wilderness areas and other natural habitats we allow them to do that fully. We do not help other creatures to praise God, but "Coming to appreciate the value they have for God raises our hearts and minds in praise to their Creator."[237]

Conclusion: Enhancing faith

So moments of awe are the rare highlights during a career in science. Scientists respond to these experiences scientifically, with new questions and investigations. They also react in other ways depending on their personalities and experience: aesthetically, using different visual representations of the data; philosophically, as they discuss the ethical implications of the research or the surprising intelligibility of the universe; or spiritually, as they try to make sense of those feelings of awe and wonder at the immensity and beauty of the world. When awe is more than simply the elation of achievement. For some scientists, the objects they study point to something else, and for Christians they lead to worship of God.

Marco Bersanelli and Mario Gargantini surveyed the writing of a huge number of scientists, looking at the motivations for their work. They found that, for those who were Christians, science more than enhanced faith: "every fragment of knowledge of the created world is an occasion for gratitude, for celebration and praise of the King of the universe". They went on to say that

> Many great scientists have expressed this praise
> of the Creator openly and in a passionate way, at
> the culmination of their scientific life, identifying
> in it the ultimate purpose and satisfaction of
> their research. Their testimony is an unusual and
> moving affirmation of Christ, Lord of the universe
> and the destiny of all things.[238]

As a final example of science leading to worship, I will quote Robert Boyle, the seventeenth-century natural philosopher and pioneer of modern chemistry:

… when with bold telescopes I survey the old and newly discovered stars and planets, that adorn the upper region of the world; and when with excellent microscopes I discern, in otherwise invisible objects, the uninimitable subtlety of nature's curious workmanship; and when, in a word, by the help of anatomical knives, and the light of chymical furnaces, I study the book of nature… I find myself oftentimes reduced to explain with the Psalmist, How manifold are Thy works, O Lord! In wisdom hast Thou made them all![239]

Chapter 9

Conversation

During the writing of this book I took a trip to the Italian Alps, also known as the Dolomites, walking 150 kilometres through some of the most beautiful and dramatic scenery I had ever seen. The mountain-savvy friend who accompanied me is a geologist and soil scientist, so I received some impromptu lessons about the rock formations we saw on the way. I learned how layers of minerals are compressed, melted, folded, and scoured by ice and rain. We saw evidence of erosion and deposition, and exclaimed at the contrast between high passes full of boulders and sheltered valleys carpeted with wild flowers.

As we walked, I began to appreciate the great age of the mountains, and imagine the processes that formed them.[240] Travelling by foot also helped me to respect their size. Looking back at the end of the day we could sometimes see exactly where we had come from: a tiny grey dot of a mountain hut perched on a blue peak in the distance. My whole body ached with fatigue from ascending and descending steep paths, carrying a rucksack that had seemed impressively light at the beginning of the trip but which now felt very heavy.

I'm not sure I can remember any of the rock names that I learned, but I can remember feeling incredibly small and insignificant compared to the long and powerful processes of plate tectonics. At the same time, I knew that the God who sustained those processes was interested in me. Time and time again, science enhances my faith.

Science is a dynamic process that involves the careful sifting of ideas, trying again and again to prove yourself wrong, always keeping an eye out for new areas of ignorance to be explored. This is a creative process, and one that requires imagination as well as tenacity. Curiosity and wonder drive the process forwards, and beauty and a deep sense of awe are the rewards for your persistence.

For a Christian, a career in science is not just compatible with faith, but it can also complement and enhance it, bringing a deeper sense of worship of the God who created everything. A scientist-believer can use their God-given creativity to the full, uncovering new areas of knowledge that increase his or her sense of wonder and awe. They can also exercise imagination, making sense of the world using all the information available to them – both scientific data and evidence from other areas of life.

One of the most important factors in this process is the ability to pay attention. If we are open to our surroundings and willing to learn new things, we will be less likely to miss that vital piece of data; that glimpse of hidden beauty; that person who has wisdom behind their ordinary-looking face. If we are open to glimpses of the transcendent, our investigations will lead us to a deeper knowledge of both God and ourselves.

The Christian faith is countercultural and full of surprises, even in the context of our present society, which is so influenced by Christian values: leaders are servants, guests are welcomed equally regardless of their social standing, no sin is worse than any other, and forgiveness is completely and utterly free. God is wise enough to come up with things that are better than we could ever imagine.

So Christians should expect the same thing to happen when they look at the world through the lens of science, and that is exactly what has happened in the last few hundred years. As Marco Bersanelli and Mario Gargantini said in their book, "Those who have faced the challenge of research know very well that nature does not obey their imagination."[241] Quantum physics, evolutionary biology, and cosmology are full of surprises that turn our theories upside down. What we observe is certainly consistent with the God that Christians believe in: a big God who surpasses all imagination.

I mentioned the technique of inference to the best explanation in chapter two, and Alister McGrath has written that

> the "best" explanation may not be the most
> reasonable or common sense explanation.
> Scientists don't lay down in advance what is
> reasonable. Time and time again, they have found
> the natural world to contradict what common
> sense might have expected or predicted. Science
> would fail if it were forced to conform to human
> ideas of rationality.

Instead, scientists must test their ideas against reality.

The instinctive question for the scientist to ask is not "Is it reasonable?" as if one knew beforehand the shape that rationality had to take, but "What makes you think that might be the case?" ... The history of science is about the recalibration of notions of "rationality" in the light of what was actually discovered about the deeper structure of nature.[242]

I find this testing of assumptions so appealing because it makes the world and our exploration of it so much more interesting. We have to go beyond our gut reactions, and that is what the people featured in this book have done. If we can leave behind the debates that spiral around and around, we may start some conversations that are more productive. We could engage across different academic fields and belief systems and become more interested in each other's ideas about the world. If we listen, we might learn from each other.

***

Over the main entrance to the Cavendish Laboratory on the West Cambridge site, which has been the home of the Department of Physics in the University of Cambridge since the early 1970s, is an inscription. "The works of the Lord are great; sought out of all them that have pleasure therein." These words are from Psalm 111, and were placed above the door at the suggestion of Andrew Briggs, now Professor of Nanomaterials at Oxford University.[243]

It is so unusual for a 1970s-era university building to include a Bible passage in its architecture, that A. B. Pippard – formerly Cavendish Professor in the University of Cambridge – explained its presence in his history of the lab:

> The great oak doors opening on the site of the
> original building had carved on them ... the text
> from Psalm 111 *Magna opera Domini exquisita*
> *in omnes voluntates ejuts.* Shortly after the move
> to the new buildings in 1973 a devout research
> student suggested to me that the same text
> should be displayed, in English, at the entrance.
> I undertook to put the proposal to the Policy
> Committee, confident that they would veto it;
> to my surprise, however, they heartily agreed
> both to the idea and to the choice of Coverdale's
> translation...[244]

This incident is the perfect example of how open-minded some science departments can be at times, and a recognition of the Christian heritage that was so important in the development of modern science. The first Cavendish Lab was established by the Scottish physicist James Clark Maxwell, and it was almost certainly he who chose the original words for the doors. For every Christian who works in that new building, and thousands of others in science around the world, this verse describes how they worship God through their work, and how science enhances their faith.

Acknowledgments

I am grateful to a large number of people who helped me to write this book. First, I want to thank the Templeton World Charity Foundation for their generous funding of this project. Then there are the six scientists who took part: Dr Harvey McMahon, Dr Ruth Hogg, Dr Jennifer Siggers, Prof Jeff Hardin, Dr Rhoda Hawkins, and Dr Robert Sluka, as well as artist Dr Lizzie Burns. I received support, ideas, information, and encouragement from the staff of The Faraday Institute for Science and Religion, many of whom also read drafts and previous incarnations in blog posts and articles, and they are: Dr Roger Abbott, Dr Denis Alexander, Dr Diana Beech, Colin Bell, Dr Zoë Binns, Lizzie Coyle, Revd Dr Rodney Holder, Dr Hilary Marlow, William McVey, Gail Pilkington, Eleanor Puttock, Dr Clare Redfern, Prof Meric Srokosz, Polly Stanton, Dr Amy Unsworth, Dr Rebecca Watson, Ben White, Prof Bob White, and Nell Whiteway. Prof Geoffrey Cook, Wei-Jin Goh, Christine Lafon, Peter Halewood, Dr Alexander Maßmann, Glenn Myers, Revd Dr Simon Perry, and Dr David Vosburg also read drafts. Abigail McFarthing helped with transcription, worship sources, and reading drafts. Dr Paul S. Anderson provided encouragement, ideas, and much-needed distraction. Numerous others, including Faraday speakers and associates, gave sources, stories, ideas, and advice. Any mistakes that remain are my own.

Acknowledgments

Previous versions of some of this content were published on scienceandbelief.org, the BioLogos forum (biologos.org/blog), the American Scientific Affiliation's *God and Nature* (godandnature.asa3.org/), and the London Institute for Contemporary Christianity's *Connecting With Culture*; in Christians in Science's *PreCiS* newsletter (www.cis.org.uk/precis-archive/), *Third Way*, *The Reader*, and *IDEA* magazine. Finally, many thanks to Tony Collins and the people from Monarch for helping me through the process of publishing this book.

Bibliography

In order to minimize the number of endnotes, I did not include one when I actually referred to a particular book. Those books are listed here.

Chapter 2: Life in the Lab

Samir Okasha, *Philosophy of Science: A Very Short Introduction*, Oxford: Oxford University Press, 2002.

John Polkinghorne, *Beyond Science: The Wider Human Context*, Cambridge: Cambridge University Press, 1996, pages 3–21.

Chapter 3: Christianity and Science

Ruth Bancewicz, *Test of FAITH: Spiritual Journeys with Scientists*, Milton Keynes: Paternoster, 2009; Eugene, OR: Wipf & Stock, 2010; Viçosa: Ultimato, 2013; Madrid: The Fliedner Foundation, 2014.

Francis Collins, *The Language of God*, New York: Free Press, 2006, page 201; London: Pocket Books, 2007.

Chapter 4: Creativity

Susan Hackwood, "Technically Creative Environments", in *Exceptional Creativity in Science and Technology: Individuals, Institutions and Innovations*, ed. Andrew Robinson, Philadelphia, PA: Templeton Press, 2013, pages 145–61.

Thomas Merton, "Theology of Creativity", in *The Literary Essays of Thomas Merton*, ed. Patrick Hart, New York: New Directions, 1981, pages 355–70.

Luci Shaw, *Breath for the Bones. Art, Imagination and Spirit: Reflections on Creativity and Faith*, Nashville, TN: Thomas Nelson, 2007.

James D. Watson, *The Double Helix*, London: Penguin, 1999 (new edition).

Articles about creativity and mobile technology

Benjamin Baird et al., "Inspired by distraction: mind wandering facilitates creative incubation", *Psychological Science* 23 (2012), pages 1117–22.

Teresa Belton & Esther Priyadharshini, "Boredom and schooling: a crossdisciplinary exploration", *Cambridge Journal of Education* 37 (2007), pages 579–95.

Brian S. Hall, "The iPhone Killed My Creativity", *Readwrite*, 29th March 2013. http://readwrite.com/2013/03/29/the-iphone-killed-my-creativity

Matt Richtel, "Silicon Valley Says Step Away From the Device", *The New York Times*, 23 July 2012. http://www.nytimes.com/2012/07/24/technology/silicon-valley-worries-about-addiction-to-devices.html?

Jessica Stillman, "Is Your Smartphone Killing Your Creativity?", *Inc.*, 3 April 2013. http://www.inc.com/jessica-stillman/is-your-smartphone-killing-your-creativity.html

Alina Tugend, "In a Constantly Plugged-In World, It's Not All Bad to Be Bored", *The New York Times*, 30 November 2012. http://www.nytimes.com/2012/12/01/your-money/why-its-not-all-bad-to-be-bored.html?

Chapter 5: Imagination

Mike Clifford, "Science and the Imagination", lecture at the Christians in Science conference, Cambridge, 2012. http://www.cis.org.uk/conferences/past-conferences/residential-2012/

Simon Conway Morris (ed.), *The Deep Structure of Biology: Is convergence sufficiently ubiquitous to give a directional signal?*, Philadelphia, PA: Templeton Foundation Press, 2008, page viii.

Richard Foster, *Celebration of Discipline: The Path to Spiritual Growth*, London: Hodder & Stoughton, 1980, pages 33–35, 38–39.

C. S. Lewis, "Bluspels & Flalansferes: A Semantic Nightmare", in *Selected Literary Essays*, ed. Walter Hooper, Cambridge: Cambridge University Press, 1969, pages 251–65.

William Loader, *The New Testament with Imagination: A Fresh Approach to its Writings and Themes*, Grand Rapids, MI: Eerdmans, 2007, page ix.

George MacDonald, "The Imagination: Its Function and its Culture", in *A Dish of Orts*, Sampson Low, Marston & Co, 1893.

James D. Watson, *The Double Helix*, London: Penguin, 1999 (new edition).

Rowan Williams, "Sinners", in Joan Chittister & Rowan Williams, *For All That Has Been, Thanks: Growing a Sense of Gratitude*, Norwich: Canterbury Press, 2010, pages 52–64.

Chapter 6: Beauty

S. Chandrasekhar, "Beauty and the Quest for Beauty in Science", Fermilab, 1979. http://history.fnal.gov/GoldenBooks/gb_chandrasekhar.html

Ursula Goodenough, *The Sacred Depths of Nature*, Oxford University Press, 1998, pages xvi &171.

Tracee Hackel, "Physics and Christian Theology: Beauty, a Common Dialect?", *Pursuit of Truth: A Journal of Christian Scholarship*, 2007. http://www.cslewis.org/journal/physics-and-christian-theology-beauty-a-common-dialect/

Jeff Hardin, "Walking the Walk: Thoreau and the art of seeing nature", *Books & Culture*, September 2013. http://www.booksandculture.com/articles/webexclusives/2013/september/walking-walk.html

Jeff Hardin, "What is the Perspective from Bioscience?", *Perspectives on Science and Christian Faith*, 53 (2001).

Gerard Manley Hopkins, "A Curious Halo", *Nature* 27 (1882).

Gerard Manley Hopkins, "Shadow-Beams in the East at Sunset", *Nature* 29 (1883).

C. S. Lewis, "The Weight of Glory", *Theology*, 43 (1941). http://tjx.sagepub.com/content/43/257/263.full.pdf+html

Jame Schaefer, "Appreciating the Beauty of the Earth", *Theological Studies* 62 (2001).

Christopher Southgate, "Looking East at Sunset: Inspiration in Art, Science and Religion", in *Inspiration in Science and Religion*, ed. Michael Fuller, Newcastle upon Tyne: Cambridge Scholars Publishing, 2012, pages 43–52.

Chapter 7: Wonder

Karl Barth, *Evangelical Theology: An Introduction*, Grand Rapids, MI: Eerdmans, 1963, pages 63–73.

Rachel Carson, *The Sense of Wonder*, Berkeley, CA: The Nature Company, 1990.

G. K. Chesterton, *Tremendous Trifles*, London: Methuen, 1909.
http://www.gutenberg.org/files/8092/8092-h/8092-h.htm

Richard Dawkins, *River Out of Eden*, London: Weidenfeld &
Nicolson, 1995.

Celia Deane-Drummond, *Wonder and Wisdom: Conversations in
Science, Spirituality, and Theology*, Philadelphia, PA: Templeton
Foundation Press, 2006.

Jürgen Moltmann, *God for a Secular Society: The Public Relevance of
Theology*, London, SCM Press, 1999, pages 149–152.

Jürgen Moltmann, *Science and Wisdom*, London, SCM Press, 2003,
pages 141–147.

Adam Smith, "The effect of unexpectedness, or of surprise" and
"Of Wonder, or of the Effects of Novelty", in *Essays on Philosophical
Subjects*, Glasgow, 1795.

Chapter 8: Awe

Richard Dawkins, *The God Delusion*, London: Black Swan, 2006,
page 406.

Calvin B. DeWitt, *Song of a Scientist: The Harmony of a God-Soaked
Creation*, Grand Rapids, MI: Square Inch, 2012.

Johannes Kepler, *The Harmony of the World*, 1619, page 1080. http://
www.sacred-texts.com/astro/how/index.htm

Notes

1 Francis Collins, *The Language of God*, New York: Free Press, 2006, page 233.

2 Nancy K. Frankenberry, *The Faith of Scientists*, Princeton & Oxford: Princeton University Press, 2008, page ix.

3 Alister E. McGrath, *Surprised by Meaning: Science, Faith, and How We Make Sense of Things*, Louisville, KY: Westminster John Knox Press, 2011.

4 Ted Davis, "Christianity and Science in Historical Perspective", *Test of FAITH* article series, www.testoffaith.com; John Hedley Brooke, *Science and Religion: Some Historical Perspectives*, Cambridge: Cambridge University Press, 1991, page 50.

5 This figure is higher than in the general population probably because in the US many Christians work at Christian universities. Figures for scientists overall give a higher percentage of believers. Ecklund's latest study of a broader group of scientists shows 24.4 per cent of scientists who are atheist/agnostic/no religious identity, compared with 15.5 per cent of the general US population. http://www.aaas.org/news/survey-symposium-inspires-hope-improved-sciencereligion-dialogue

6 Elaine Howard Ecklund, "Scientists and Spirituality", *Sociology of Religion* 0 (2011), pages 1–22; Elaine Howard Ecklund, *Science vs. Religion: What Scientists Really Think*, Oxford: Oxford University Press, 2010, pages 51–68.

7 "Setting the agenda", http://www.testoffaith.com/resources/resource.aspx?id=274

8 Marco Bersanelli & Mario Gargantini, *From Galileo to Gell-Mann: The Wonder That Inspired the Greatest Scientists of All Time*, Philadelphia, PA: Templeton Press, 2009, page 104.

9   "Jocelyn Bell Burnell", in *Beautiful Minds*, The British Broadcasting Company, 2010.

10 The last two years of secondary school, as they were called in England in the early nineties.

11 Stuart Firestein, *Ignorance: How it Drives Science*, New York: Oxford University Press, 2012, page 176.

12 Eve Curie, *Madame Curie: Discoverer of Radium*, translated by Vincent Sheean, London: Heinemann, 1939, page 179.

13 Andy Crouch, *Culture Making: Recovering our Creative Calling*, Downers Grove, IL: IVP, 2008, pages 249–51.

14 Scientists used to be called natural philosophers, so PhD is short for the antiquated but grand title, "doctor of philosophy". Just to be different, some universities call the same qualification a DPhil.

15 Firestein, *Ignorance: How it Drives Science*, pages 1–9; Stuart Firestein, "Certainly not!" *Nautilus*, issue 2, 6 June 2013. nautil.us/issue/2/uncertainty/certainly-not; Stuart Firestein, "The Pursuit of Ignorance", *TED talk*, September 2013. http://www.ted.com/talks/stuart_firestein_the_pursuit_of_ignorance.html

16 Firestein, *Ignorance: How it Drives Science*, page 4

17 Firestein, *Ignorance: How it Drives Science*, page 7

18 François Jacob, *Of Flies, Mice, and Men*, Cambridge, MA: Harvard University Press, 1998, page 126.

19 Steven Johnson, author of *Where Good Ideas Come From: The Natural History of Innovation*, London: Penguin, 2010. http://www.youtube.com/watch?feature=player_embedded&v=eNwMut3-z1Y

20 Jacob, *The Statue Within: An Autobiography*, translated by Franklin Philip, page 296.

21 Peter B. Medawar, *The Art of the Soluble*, Harmondsworth: Penguin, 1969, pages 127–43.

22 Atoms are the smallest component of matter, e.g. Hydrogen and Oxygen. Molecules are collections of atoms, e.g. H_2O. Atoms *can* be divided into smaller components, but that involves very violent forces.

22 Based on Denis R. Alexander, lecture on "The Christian Roots of Science", Launde Abbey, Leicestershire, June 2013.

24 John Polkinghorne, *Beyond Science: The Wider Human Context*, Cambridge: Cambridge University Press, 1996, pages 3–21.

Notes

25   McGrath, *Surprised by Meaning*, page 2.

26   A more elegant version of this quote, "Let your religion be less of a theory and more of a love affair", has often been used but I find it untraceable, and suspect that it is a paraphrase. This version is from G. K. Chesterton, *St Francis of Assisi*, 1957, chapter 1. http://gutenberg.net.au/ebooks09/0900611.txt

27   W. K. Clifford, "The Ethics of Belief", *Contemporary Review* (1877), http://infidels.org/library/historical/w_k_clifford/ethics_of_belief.html

28   If it is possible to *prove* anything scientifically. As I explained in the previous chapter, science is about evidence, and maths is about proof – so logical statements like these are not really open to scientific investigation.

29   C. S. Lewis, "The Language of Religion", in *Christian Reflections*, Bles, 1967. Latest edition Grand Rapids: Eerdmans 1994, page 164.

30   Ian Sample, "Martin Rees: I've got no religious beliefs at all – interview", *The Guardian,* 6 April 2011. http://www.theguardian.com/science/2011/apr/06/astronomer-royal-martin-rees-interview

31   C. S. Lewis, "Is Theology Poetry?" in *Screwtape Proposes a Toast, and Other Pieces*, London: Fontana, 1965, page 58.

32   McGrath, *Surprised by Meaning*, pages 22–29.

33   Preliminary data from a survey by Professor Elaine Howard Ecklund. http://www.aaas.org/sites/default/files/content_files/RU_AAASPresentationNotes_2014_0219%20%281%29.pdf

34   Noah Efron, "That Christianity gave birth to modern science" in ed. Ronald Numbers, *Galileo Goes to Jail and Other Myths About Science and Religion,* Cambridge, MA: Harvard University Press, 2009, pages 78–89.

35   After this, science began to die out in the Islamic world for a while and scholars have not been able to agree why.

36   Psalm 93:1, *The Holy Bible, English Standard Version*, Crossway Bibles, 2001.

37   "A Survey of Clergy and Their Views on Origins", *The BioLogos Forum*, 8 May 2013. http://biologos.org/blog/a-survey-of-clergy-and-their-views-on-origins

38   This diagram is not to scale, and misses out many activities, so it is not intended to illustrate a balanced life!

39   E. O. Wilson, "On the Origin of the Arts", *Harvard Magazine* (May–June 2012), pages 32–37. (Reproduced from his book, *The Social Conquest of Earth*, W. W. Norton, 2012, pages 268–86.)

40   Thomas Merton, "Theology of Creativity", in *The Literary Essays of Thomas Merton*, ed. Patrick Hart, New York: New Directions, 1981, pages 355–70.

41   Creative thinking, or solving problems by viewing them from an unusual angle.

42   Partly because a "gene" is not a discrete entity, but broken up into chunks. There might be some "alternative splicing" – chunks that are only used at certain times, and are swapped in when needed. The concept of a gene is still useful, but molecular biologists now know that the real picture is more complicated than "one gene, one protein".

43   My lecturer may have been referring to the Hepatitis E virus, or the Sendai Virus. Curran & Kolakofsky, "Sendai virus P gene produces multiple proteins from overlapping open reading frames", *Enzyme* 44 (1990), pages 244–49.

44   Sanna, Li & Zhang, "Overlapping genes in the human and mouse genomes", *BMC Genomics* 9 (2008), page 169.

45   A "genome" is the total amount of DNA for any organism.

46   Catie Lichten, "Meaning over Money", *Research*, 20 June 2013. http://www.researchresearch.com/index.php?option=com_news &template=rr_2col&view=article&articleId=1336296

47   Susan Hackwood, "Technically Creative Environments", in *Exceptional Creativity in Science and Technology: Individuals, Institutions and Innovations*, ed. Andrew Robinson, Philadelphia, PA: Templeton Press, 2013, pages 145–61.

48   *Shorter Oxford English Dictionary*, Oxford: the Clarendon Press, 1975.

49   Hilary Brand & Adrienne Chaplin, *Art and Soul: Signposts for Christians in the Arts*, Carlisle: Piquant, 2001, pages 93–95.

50   Brand & Chaplin, *Art and Soul: Signposts for Christians in the Arts*, pages 93–95.

51   John Hope Mason, *The Value of Creativity: The Origins and Emergence of a Modern Belief*, Aldershot, Hants: Ashgate, 2003, pages 1–11.

Notes

52   Philip West, "Divine Creation and Human Creativity", *New Blackfriars*, 67 (1986), pages 478–84; Hope Mason, *The Value of Creativity: The Origins and Emergence of a Modern Belief*, pages 1–11.

53   Margaret Boden, "Précis of The Creative Mind: Myths and Mechanisms", *Behavioural and Brain Sciences* 17 (1994), pages 519–70.

54   Jacob Bronowski, *Science and Human Values*, London: Faber & Faber, 2008 (first published 1956), pages 1–30.

55   Margaret Boden, "Précis of The Creative Mind: Myths and Mechanisms", *Behavioural and Brain Sciences*, pages 519–70.

56   Ann Loades, *Dorothy L. Sayers: Spiritual Writings*, London: SPCK, 1993, pages 82–87.

57   Paul Alexander, *Creativity in Worship*, London: Daybreak, 1990, pages 1–11.

58   IQ tests measure linguistic ability, spatial awareness, speed of thinking, and memory. Alan S. Kaufman, *IQ testing 101*, New York: Springer, 2009.

59   Jessica Stillman, "John Cleese: Busyness Is the Enemy of Creativity", *CBS News*, 20 September 2010. http://www.cbsnews.com/8301-505125_162-38943169/john-cleese-busyness-is-the-enemy-of-creativity/

60   Steven Johnson, "Where good ideas come from", 21 September 2012. http://www.youtube.com/watch?feature=player_embedded&v=eNwMut3-z1Y

61   Zella King, "Genius networks: Link to a more creative social circle", *New Scientist*, 2866 (2012), pages 37–39.

62   I'd say "life cycle", but viruses are not always considered to be living organisms because they don't have cells, and can't reproduce on their own.

63   Cold Spring Harbor and the phage course: http://www.cshl.edu/About-Us/History/ & http://symposium.cshlp.org/site/misc/topic18.xhtml

64   This analogy comes from Donald Mackay, author of *The Clockwork Image: A Christian Perspective on Science*, Leicester: IVP, new edition 1997.

65   Samaritans worshipped God on Mount Gerizim, and the Jews worshipped in Jerusalem. The two groups were at odds (to say the least), and most Jews would avoid going into Samaritan territory.

66   Mark Bozzuti-Jones, "In God's Image: A Theology of
      Creativity", 16 April 2009. http://www.trinitywallstreet.org/
      content/gods-image-theology-creativity
67   David Wilkinson, *The Message of Creation*, Leicester:
      InterVarsity Press, 2002, pages 31–45.
68   Loades, *Dorothy L. Sayers: Spiritual Writings*, page 82. (Also in
      "Towards a Christian Aesthetic", in *Unpopular Opinions*.)
69   Dorothy L. Sayers, *The Mind of the Maker*, London: Methuen,
      1942, page 17.
70   J. R .R. Tolkien, *The Silmarillion*, "Of Aulë and Yavanna",
      from David Vosburg, "The Personal Journey of a Faith-Filled
      Scientist", *The BioLogos Forum*, 24 September 2013. http://
      biologos.org/blog/the-personal-journey-of-a-faith-filled-scientist
71   Brand & Chaplin, *Art and Soul: Signposts for Christians in the
      Arts*, pages 42–47.
72   J. Richard Middleton, *The Liberating Image: The Imago Dei in
      Genesis 1*, Grand Rapids, IL: Baker Publishing, 2005, pages
      287–89, 296–97.
73   Denis R. Alexander, "Worshipping God with Technology",
      Cambridge Papers 12 (2003).
74   Exodus 25:34; 31:1–11; 35:30–35.
75   1 Kings 6; 1 Chronicles 28 – 2 Chronicles 4.
76   Poetry, e.g. 2 Samuel 23:1–2; Music, e.g. Numbers 10; Song,
      e.g. Deuteronomy 31:19; Psalm 40:3; Monument, e.g. Joshua
      4; Clothes, Exodus 28; Prophetic performance, e.g. Isaiah 20;
      Jeremiah 19, 27, 28; Ezekiel 4, 5. Brand & Chaplin, *Art and
      Soul: Signposts for Christians in the Arts*, page 42.
77   Alexander, "Worshipping God with Technology".
78   Bozzuti-Jones, "In God's Image: A Theology of Creativity".
79   Andy Crouch, "Delight in Creation: The Life of a Scientist",
      Perspectives on Science and Christian Belief, 66 (2014), pages 40–46.
80   Andy Crouch, *Culture Making: Recovering our Creative Calling*,
      pages 97–98.
81   Peter Medawar, *Pluto's Republic* (incorporating *The Art of the
      Soluble* & *Induction in Scientific Thought*), Oxford: Oxford
      University Press, 1982, page 108.
82   Mary Midgley, *Science and Poetry*, London: Routledge, 2001, page 1.
83   An organization for those interested in the interaction between

Notes

science and Christianity. www.cis.org.uk

84   Douglas Hedley, *Living Forms of the Imagination*, London: T&T Clark, 2008, pages 2–3.

85   Michael Ferber, *Romanticism: A Very Short Introduction*, Oxford: Oxford University Press, 2010, pages xiii-xiv, 63–92.

86   Gerald Holton, "On the art of scientific imagination", *Daedalus* 125 (1996), pages 183–208; Mary Midgley, *Science and Poetry*, pages 47–58.

87   *The Compact Oxford English Dictionary*, Oxford: Clarendon Press, 1991.

88   Hedley, *Living Forms of the Imagination*, pages 39–78.

89   Sandra Levy, *Imagination and the Journey of Faith*, Grand Rapids, IL: Eerdmans, 2008, pages 9–10.

90   Trevor Hart, "Creative Imagination and Moral Identity", *Studies in Christian Ethics* 16 (2003), pages 1–13.

91   C.L.O.C.K. stands for Circadian Locomotor Output Cycles Kaput. Genetic acronyms tend to be creative!

92   Peter Medawar, *The Limits of Science*, Oxford: Oxford University Press, 1986, pages 45–52, 83–87.

93   "The Role of Thought Experiments in Science and Theology" lecture by Prof Niels Gregersen, *The Faraday Institute Seminar Series*, 19 February 2013. http://www.faraday.st-edmunds.cam. ac.uk/Multimedia.php?Mode=Add&ItemID=Item_Multimedia _507&width=720&height=460

94   Hedley, *Living Forms of the Imagination*, pages 65–68.

95   Medawar, *The Limits of Science*, page 51.

96   A helpful explanation of imaginary numbers can be found at http://www.mathopenref.com/imaginary-number.html

97   Mike Clifford, "Science and the Imagination", lecture at the Christians in Science conference, Cambridge, 2012. http:// www.cis.org.uk/conferences/past-conferences/residential-2012/

98   I could say that when I wear my jeans to church, they are a symbol of God being in the midst of my everyday life.

99   John McIntyre, *Faith, Theology and Imagination*, Edinburgh: The Handsel Press, 1987, pages 19–28.

100   John McIntyre, *Faith, Theology and Imagination*, pages 56–61.

101   Holton, "On the art of scientific imagination", *Daedalus*, pages 183–208.

102   Hedley, *Living Forms of the Imagination*, page 3.

103   Hedley, *Living Forms of the Imagination*, page 5.

104   Hedley, *Living Forms of the Imagination*, page 5.

105   Hedley, *Living Forms of the Imagination*, pages 73–74.

106   Hedley, *Living Forms of the Imagination*, page 3; McIntyre,
      Faith, Theology and the Imagination, pages 4–11.

107   Kerry Dearborn, "The Baptised Imagination", in *Inklings of
      Glory. Christian Reflection: A Series in Faith and Ethics*, ed.
      Robert B. Krushwitz, Waco: Baylor University, 2004, page 11.
      http://www.baylor.edu/christianethics/index.php?id=17455

108   Dearborn, "The Baptised Imagination", in *Inklings of Glory.
      Christian Reflection: A Series in Faith and Ethics*, page 11.

109   Dearborn, "The Baptised Imagination", in *Inklings of Glory.
      Christian Reflection: A Series in Faith and Ethics*, page 12.

110   Dearborn, "The Baptised Imagination", in *Inklings of Glory.
      Christian Reflection: A Series in Faith and Ethics*, page 13.

111   George MacDonald, "The Imagination: Its Function and its
      Culture", in *A Dish of Orts*, Sampson Low, Marston & Co, 1897.

112   Francis Schaeffer, *Art & the Bible*, Downers Grove, IL:
      InterVarsity Press, 1973, page 91.

113   Hedley, *Living Forms of the Imagination*, pages 47–49; Richard
      Dawkins, *Unweaving the Rainbow*, Allen Lane, 1998; Boston:
      Houghton Mifflin, 1998, pages 257–85.

114   Apoptosis is the Greek word describing the way that petals or
      leaves drop off a plant. In J. F. R. Kerr, A. H. Wyllie & A. R.
      Currie, *Br. J. Cancer*, 26 (1972).

115   Andrew Wyllie, "How and Why Cells Die – Biological and
      Theological Perspectives", *Faraday Institute Seminar Series*, 25
      January 2011. http://www.faraday.st-edmunds.cam.ac.uk/
      Multimedia.php?Mode=Add&ItemID=Item_Multimedia_391
      &width=720&height=460

116   Paleobiologists study fossils, investigating how they relate to
      present-day living things and ecosystems.

117   All scientific articles are anonymously reviewed by other experts
      in the field.

118   *Test of FAITH: Does Science Threaten Belief in God?* (DVD,
      Milton Keynes: Paternoster, 2009; Eugene, OR: Wipf &
      Stock, 2010; Viçosa: Ultimato, 2013; Madrid: The Fliedner

Notes

Foundation, 2014); also in "A Random Process?" http://www.
testoffaith.com/resources/resource.aspx?id=432

119 Blaise Pascal, *Pensées*, number 72. http://www.gutenberg.org/
files/18269/18269-h/18269-h.htm

120 Bersanelli & Gargantini, *From Galileo to Gell-Mann: The
Wonder That Inspired the Greatest Scientists of All Time*, page 9.

121 Alister McGrath, *The Open Secret: A New Vision for Natural
Theology*, Oxford: Blackwell, 2008, pages 1–2.

122 http://www.nature.com/ncb/journal/v2/n12/index.html#ed

123 Lizzie isn't a believer in God herself, but was fascinated by this
project and willing to be interviewed for it. Her work can be
found at http://www.sciencetolife.org/html/staff.html, http://
www.molecular-designs.com/html/dr_lizzie_burns.html and
https://www.flickr.com/photos/drlizzieburns/

124 Human development is so complex and our bodies are so large
and vary so much in size that estimates vary from 10 to 100
trillion. Our bodies and digestive tracts are also covered in
trillions of (useful) yeast and bacterial cells.

125 Except the eggs and sperm, which have variable cell numbers.

126 Roger Scruton, *Beauty: A Very Short Introduction*, Oxford
University Press, 2011, pages 1–28; Crispin Sartwell, "Beauty",
ed. Edward N. Zalta, *Stanford Encyclopaedia of Philosophy*
(Spring 2014 Edition), http://plato.stanford.edu/archives/
spr2014/entries/beauty/

127 Richard Viladesau, *Theological Aesthetics: God in Imagination,
Beauty, and Art*, Oxford University Press, 1999, pages 8–11;
Paul Guyer, "18th Century German Aesthetics", ed. Edward
N. Zalta, *The Stanford Encyclopedia of Philosophy* (Fall 2008
Edition), http://plato.stanford.edu/archives/fall2008/entries/
aesthetics-18th-german/.

128 E. O. Wilson, "On the Origin of the Arts", *Harvard Magazine*
(May–June 2012), pages 32–37. (Reproduced from his book,
The Social Conquest of Earth, New York: W. W. Norton, 2012,
pages 268–86); Noël Carroll, "On Being Moved by Nature:
Between Religion and Natural History" in eds. Alex Neill &
Aaron Ridley, *Arguing About Art: Contemporary Philosophical
Debates*, McGraw-Hill, Inc., 1995, pages 139–60.

129 Translations vary. We have used the version from Albert
     Einstein, ed., *Living Philosophies*, New York, Simon & Schuster,
     1931.

130 Denis R. Alexander, "Truth and Beauty in Science", lecture at
     the C. S. Lewis Symposium, Cambridge, 2008. I have taken
     some points from this lecture and adapted them to produce my
     own categories of beauty in science.

131 Jürgen Moltmann, "From Physics to Theology: A Personal
     Story", *The Faraday Institute Lecture Series*, 14 February 2012.
     http://www.faraday.st-edmunds.cam.ac.uk/Multimedia.
     php?Mode=Add&ItemID=Item_Multimedia_458&width=720
     &height=460

132 James Turner, "Mathematics and Beauty", in *Delight in
     Creation*, Deborah Haarsma & Scott Hoezee, The Ministry
     Theorem, 2012, pages 157–81: http://ministrytheorem.
     calvinseminary.edu/essays/wiwmpk/; Robert M. May "Beauty
     and Truth: their intersection in mathematics and science", in
     eds. Lauren Arrington, Zoë Leinhardt & Philip Dawid *Beauty:
     The Darwin College Lectures*, Cambridge University Press, 2013,
     pages 6–25.

133 Peter Goddard, ed., *Paul Dirac: The Man and His Work*,
     Cambridge University Press, 1998, page 89.

134 Holton, "On the art of scientific imagination", *Daedalus*, pages
     183–208.

135 Bersanelli & Gargantini, *From Galileo to Gell-Mann: The
     Wonder That Inspired the Greatest Scientists of All Time*, page 13.

136 Bersanelli & Gargantini, *From Galileo to Gell-Mann: The
     Wonder That Inspired the Greatest Scientists of All Time*, page 6.

137 "Fathers of the Church", in ed. E.A. Livingstone, *The Concise
     Oxford Dictionary of the Christian Church* (2nd Revised
     Edition), Oxford University Press, 2006.

138 Not every theologian wrote about each level, but all five ways of
     appreciating nature are common among their writings.

139 Of course Jesus is God, and was visible.

140 I borrowed this title from a book about the medieval
     contribution to science: James Hannam, *God's Philosophers:
     How the Medieval World Laid the Foundations of Modern*

Notes

Science, London: Icon Books, 2010; in the US, *The Genesis of Science: How the Christian Middle Ages Launched the Scientific Revolution*, Regnery Press, 2011.

141 R. J. Berry, "The Research Scientist's Psalm", *Science & Christian Belief* 20 (2008), pages 160–61.

142 Frankenberry, *The Faith of Scientists,* page 43.

143 "John Ray, Life and Times", *The John Ray Initiative*. http://www.jri.org.uk/ray/index.htm

144 John Meurig Thomas, "The Genius of Michael Faraday", *Faraday Institute Seminar Series*, 20 November 2012; Colin Russell, "Science and Faith in the Life of Michael Faraday", *Faraday Papers* 13 (2007). http://www.faraday.st-edmunds.cam.ac.uk/Papers.php

145 The oldest scientific society in the world.

146 Michael Faraday, lecture notes from 1858, quoted in Bence Jones, *The Life and Letters of Faraday* (1870) Vol. 2, page 404. http://quod.lib.umich.edu/m/moa/AJN6604.0002.001?view=toc

147 Faraday, quoted in Bence Jones, *The Life and Letters of Faraday*, page 404.

148 Russell, "Science and Faith in the Life of Michael Faraday", *Faraday Papers* 13.

149 Russell, "Science and Faith in the Life of Michael Faraday", *Faraday Papers* 13.

150 Viladesau, *Theological Aesthetics: God in Imagination, Beauty and Art*, page 12.

151 Jame Schaefer, *Theological Foundations for Environmental Ethics: Reconstructing Patristic & Medieval Concepts*, Washington, DC: Georgetown University Press, 2009, page 68.

152 Simplified from McGrath, *The Open Secret: A New Vision for Natural Theology*, pages 59–79.

153 McGrath, *The Open Secret: A New Vision for Natural Theology*, pages 1–2.

154 Rodney Holder, *The Heavens Declare: Natural Theology and the Legacy of Karl Barth*, Philadelphia, PA: Templeton Press, 2012.

155 McGrath, *The Open Secret: A New Vision for Natural Theology*, page 209.

156 Though I suspect I would disagree with much of the rest of his theology.

157 Viladesau, *Theological Aesthetics: God in Imagination, Beauty and Art*, page 12.

158 Viladesau, *Theological Aesthetics: God in Imagination, Beauty and Art*.

159 Tracee Hackel, "Physics and Christian Theology: Beauty, a Common Dialect?" *Pursuit of Truth: A Journal of Christian Scholarship*, 2007. http://www.cslewis.org/journal/physics-and-christian-theology-beauty-a-common-dialect/

160 McGrath, *The Open Secret: A New Vision for Natural Theology*, pages 262–63.

161 Viladesau, *Theological Aesthetics: God in Imagination, Beauty and Art*, pages 25–35, quote page 33.

162 Schaefer, *Theological Foundations for Environmental Ethics: Reconstructing Patristic & Medieval Concepts*, pages 68–69.

163 Schaefer, *Theological Foundations for Environmental Ethics: Reconstructing Patristic & Medieval Concepts*, pages 68–69.

164 J. Williams, "Symmetry in Science", *Bluesci* (The Cambridge University Science Magazine), 2012; Nina Byers, "E. Noether's Discovery of the Deep Connection Between Symmetries and Conservation Law", *Israel Mathematical Conference Proceedings*, 12 (1999). http://cwp.library.ucla.edu/articles/noether.asg/noether.html

165 McGrath, *The Open Secret: A New Vision for Natural Theology*, page 70.

166 I borrowed this concept from Shannon Stahl (see chapter eight), who has this feeling when his ideas come together in a grant application.

167 It looks as though Lewis is making a reference to Hebrews 12:14–16

168 Veronica van Heyningen, "Gene games of the Future" (Book Review), *Nature* 408 (2000).

169 Jürgen Moltmann, *God for a Secular Society: The Public Relevance of Theology*, London: SCM Press, 1999, page 161.

170 References for this section: a variety of dictionaries; Celia Deane-Drummond, *Wonder and Wisdom: Conversations in*

Science, Spirituality and Theology, Philadelphia, PA: Templeton Foundation Press, 2006, pages 1–6; eds. R. J. W. Evans and Alexander Marr, *Curiosity and Wonder from the Renaissance to the Enlightenment*, London: Ashgate, 2006; Christopher Southgate, *God, Humanity and the Cosmos*, London: T & T Clark, 2005, pages 67 & 70; Lorraine Daston & Katharine Park, *Wonders and the Order of Nature*, New York: Zone Books, 2001.

171 McGrath, *The Open Secret: A New Vision for Natural Theology*, pages 226, 277–80.

172 See chapter five.

173 Deane-Drummond, *Wonder and Wisdom: Conversations in Science, Spirituality and Theology*, pages 5–7.

174 Richard Dawkins, *Unweaving the Rainbow*, page 6.

175 Dawkins, *Unweaving the Rainbow*, page 7.

176 Anthony T. Annunziato, "DNA Packaging: Nucleosomes and Chromatin", *Nature Education* (1), 2008. http://www.nature.com/scitable/topicpage/dna-packaging-nucleosomes-and-chromatin-310

177 Margaret Boden, "Wonder and Understanding", *Zygon* 20 (1985), pages 391–400.

178 Bersanelli & Gargantini, *From Galileo to Gell-Mann: The Wonder That Inspired the Greatest Scientists of All Time*, page 155.

179 Olaf Pedersen, "Christian belief and the fascination of science" in eds. Robert John Russell, William R. Stoeger & George V. Coyne, *Physics, Philosophy and Theology: A Common Quest for Understanding*, Vatican City State: Vatican Observatory, 1988, pages 125–40.

180 Bersanelli & Gargantini, *From Galileo to Gell-Mann: The Wonder That Inspired the Greatest Scientists of All Time*, page 8.

181 Einstein's beliefs are described by Max Jammer, *Einstein and Religion: Physics and Theology*, Princeton: Princeton University Press, 1999, pages 67–75; Heisenberg's by Enrico Cantore, *Scientific Man: The Humanistic Significance of Science*, ISH Publications, 1977, pages 117–18; Rachel Carson was deeply spiritual but didn't hold to any particular religion, and she did believe in God, see Frankenberry, *The Faith of Scientists*, pages 197–221; I can find no evidence of Carlo Rubbia's views about God.

182 See chapter one.

183 Ruth Bancewicz, *Test of FAITH: Spiritual Journeys with Scientists* (Milton Keynes: Paternoster, 2009; Eugene, OR: Wipf & Stock, 2010; Viçosa: Ultimato, 2013; Madrid: The Fliedner Foundation, 2014), pages 43–44.

184 Alister E. McGrath, "Has Science Eliminated God?", *Science and Christian Belief* 17 (2005), pages 115–35.

185 Richard Dawkins, *Unweaving the Rainbow*, page x

186 McGrath, "Has Science Eliminated God?", *Science and Christian Belief*, pages 115–35.

187 Deane-Drummond, *Wonder and Wisdom: Conversations in Science, Spirituality and Theology*.

188 Celia Deane-Drummond, "Experiencing Wonder and Seeking Wisdom", *Zygon* 42 (2007), pages 587–90.

189 John Polkinghorne, *Beyond Science: The Wider Human Context*, pages 103–112.

190 Scott E. Hoezee, *Proclaim the Wonder: Engaging Science on Sunday*, Grand Rapids, MI: Baker, 2003, pages 67–70.

191 For wonder and awe respectively: NIV 109 and 53 times, ESV 80 and 47, NLT 181 and 60, NASB 104 and 42, Good News 123 and 26. More versions are available on http://www.biblegateway.com/

192 Matthew, Mark, Luke, and John.

193 Particularly in the book of Acts.

194 The quotes below are from Jürgen Moltmann, *Science and Wisdom*, London: SCM Press, 2003, pages 141–47 and Jürgen Moltmann, *God for a Secular Society: The Public Relevance of Theology*, pages 149–52.

195 Richard Dawkins, *The Magic of Reality*, London: Bantam Press, 2011, page 16.

196 McGrath, "Has Science Eliminated God?", *Science and Christian Belief*, page 131.

197 Glen G. Scorgie, "Wonder and the Revitalisation of Theology", *Crux* 26 (1990), page 22.

198 Moltmann, *God for a Secular Society: The Public Relevance of Theology*, page 161.

199 Bersanelli & Gargantini, *From Galileo to Gell-Mann: The Wonder That Inspired the Greatest Scientists of All Time*, page 7.

Notes

200 See the beginning of chapter four for an introduction to DNA.

201 P. Turner, A. G. McLennan, M. R. H. White, *Molecular Biology, Third Edition*, New York: Taylor & Francis, 2005, electronic edition, page 91.

202 Jeff Hardin, Gregory Bertoni, Lewis J. Kleinsmith, *Becker's World of the Cell*, San Francisco: Benjamin Cummings, 2012, page 550. The replication phase is six to eight hours. The human genome is 3,200,000,000 subunits long. You do the maths!

203 Not to be confused with overhead projector transparencies, for those of us old enough to remember them.

204 Which was discovered through several decades of careful research by a large number of people. The main players in the discovery were Hans Krebs and Albert Szent-Györgyi, and they earned a Nobel Prize for their efforts. I think I know why this particular pathway was named after only one of the discoverers… A Bancewicz cycle is also unlikely, although the fact that I have left the lab won't help either.

205 That's almost every animal, and many bacteria.

206 McGrath, *The Open Secret: A New Vision for Natural Theology*, page 226.

207 Guy Ottewell, "The Thousand-Yard Model", 1989. http://www.noao.edu/education/peppercorn/pcmain.html

208 Cantore, *Scientific Man: The Humanistic Significance of Science*, page 109.

209 Cantore, *Scientific Man: The Humanistic Significance of Science*, page 110.

210 Bersanelli & Gargantini, *From Galileo to Gell-Mann: The Wonder That Inspired the Greatest Scientists of All Time*, page 6.

211 "True Science", review of Peter Medawar's *Advice to a Young Scientist* (1980), *The London Review of Books* (Mar 1981), page 6.

212 Enrique Mota, "Modelling Reality", *Science and Belief*, 14 June 2012. http://scienceandbelief.org/2012/06/14/modelling-reality/#more-1317

213 Albert Einstein, "Principles of Research", address to the Physical Society, Berlin, for Max Planck's sixtieth birthday, 1918. http://www.site.uottawa.ca/~yymao/misc/Einstein_PlanckBirthday.html

214 US News & World Report, 23 December 1991.

215 Bersanelli & Gargantini, *From Galileo to Gell-Mann: The Wonder That Inspired the Greatest Scientists of All Time*, page 7.

216 Celia Deane-Drummond, *Wonder and Wisdom: Conversations in Science, Spirituality and Theology*, pages 138–39.

217 Albert Einstein, *My Credo*, recorded for the German League of Human Rights, 1932. http://www.einstein-website.de/z_biography/credo.html

218 Cantore, *Scientific Man: The Humanistic Significance of Science*, page 114.

219 McGrath, *The Open Secret: A New Vision for Natural Theology*, pages 28–33.

220 Olaf Pedersen, "Christian belief and the fascination of science" in *Physics, Philosophy and Theology: A Common Quest for Understanding*, page 133.

221 Cantore, *Scientific Man: The Humanistic Significance of Science*, page 120.

222 Albert Einstein, *My Credo*, recorded for the German League of Human Rights, 1932.

223 Shannon Stahl, "Faith and Chemistry", *Science and Belief*, 27 October 2011.

224 Jame Schaefer, "Appreciating the Beauty of the Earth", *Theological Studies* 62 (2001).

225 As described in John chapter 1.

226 Mentioned in chapter seven.

227 Resources on this topic can be found at http://www.arocha.org/ke-en/work/research/marine/faith.html, or email Bob at bob.sluka@arocha.org

228 See chapter six.

229 See chapter six for my previous mention of John Ray. I have been unable to find a source for this Cambridge anecdote, but it is consistent with the personality of John Ray, as seen in his published writing.

230 Personal communication, cited with permission. For more about her work and faith, see "Meditation on Light", *The BioLogos Forum*, 8 August 2010. http://biologos.org/blog/meditation-on-light

231 Fernando Caballero, "Greatest in the Small Things", *Science and Belief*, 13 September 2012.

Notes

232 Andy Crouch, *Culture Making: Recovering our Creative Calling*, pages 166–70; Alexander, "Worshipping God with Technology".

233 Georgina Ferry, "Life in Stone", *Nature* 489 (2012). http://www.stmaryswreay.org/

234 "Where are the Voyagers?" http://voyager.jpl.nasa.gov/where/

235 Jennifer Wiseman, "Science as an Instrument of Worship: Can recent scientific discovery inform and inspire our worship and service?" *BioLogos Essay Series*, November 2009. http://biologos.org/resources/essay/science-as-an-instrument-of-worship

236 Matt Redman, *Facedown*, Eastbourne: Survivor, 2004, page 29.

237 Richard Bauckham, "Loving our Fellow Creatures: Christians and Animal Rights", *Anglican Society for the Welfare of Animals*, by permission of Scripture Union. http://www.aswa.org.uk/page/articles/loving_our_fellow_creatures/

238 Bersanelli & Gargantini, *From Galileo to Gell-Mann: The Wonder That Inspired the Greatest Scientists of All Time*, page 248.

239 Bersanelli & Gargantini, *From Galileo to Gell-Mann: The Wonder That Inspired the Greatest Scientists of All Time*, page 249.

240 There is an excellent account of how geology changed the way we see mountains in Robert Macfarlane's *Mountains of the Mind: A History of a Fascination*, London: Granta Books, 2003, pages 22–65.

241 Bersanelli & Gargantini, *From Galileo to Gell-Mann: The Wonder That Inspired the Greatest Scientists of All Time*, page 4.

242 McGrath, *Surprised by Meaning: Science, Faith, and How we Make Sense of Things*, page 27.

243 Andrew Briggs, "And Information Became Physical", in ed. R. J. Berry, *True Scientists, True Faith*, Monarch, 2014, in press.

244 A. B. Pippard, "The Cavendish Laboratory", *Eur.J. Physics*, 8 (1987), page 235.

Index

Index

Index